Seven Testimonies of God

The Evidence Speaks for Itself

Take your faith where the evidence leads!

This is observational science, logic, evidence and Divine design!

By

Charles Richard Gerber MA; LMHC
Christian Counseling Services
1804 North Wheeling Ave.
Suite 5
Muncie, IN 47303

Is your faith based on evidence, or is it "blind faith"?

All the Bible passages are New International Version, unless stated otherwise.

The opinions expressed in this manuscript are those of the author and do not necessarily represent the thoughts or opinions of the publisher. The author warrants and represents that he has the legal right to publish or own all material in this book. If you find a discrepancy, contact the publisher at www.avidreaderspg.com.

Seven Testimonies of God

All Rights Reserved

Copyright © 2018 Charles Richard Gerber MA

This book may not be transmitted, reproduced, or stored in part or in whole by any means without the express written consent of the publisher except for brief quotations in articles and reviews.

Avid Readers Publishing Group

http://www.avidreaderspg.com

ISBN-13: 978-1-61286-341-2

Printed in the United States

From a great dialogue…   A man in the crowd answered, "Teacher, I brought you my son, who is possessed by a spirit that has robbed him of speech. 18 Whenever it seizes him, it throws him to the ground. He foams at the mouth, gnashes his teeth and becomes rigid. I asked your disciples to drive out the spirit, but they could not."

19 "O unbelieving generation," Jesus replied, "how long shall I stay with you? How long shall I put up with you? Bring the boy to me."

20 So they brought him. When the spirit saw Jesus, it immediately threw the boy into a convulsion. He fell to the ground and rolled around, foaming at the mouth.

21 Jesus asked the boy's father, "How long has he been like this?"

"From childhood," he answered. 22 "It has often thrown him into fire or water to kill him. But if you can do anything, take pity on us and help us."

23 "'If you can'?" said Jesus. "Everything is possible for him who believes."

24 Immediately the boy's father exclaimed, "I do believe; help me overcome my unbelief!"

Mark 9:17-24

> "I do believe, help me overcome my unbelief." What a great statement. This is what this Bible study is designed to do when it comes to God. To overcome your unbelief!

Patrick Glynn, in his book <u>God: The Evidence</u>, writes that everything had to be "'just right' from the very start—everything from the values of fundamental forces like electromagnetism and gravity, to the relative masses of the various subatomic particles, to things like the number of neutrino types at time 1 second, which the universe has to 'know' already at 10-43 second. The slightest tinkering with a single one of scores of basic values and relationships in nature would have resulted in a universe very different from the one we inhabit—say, one with no stars like our sun, or no stars, period. Far from being accidental, life appeared to be the goal toward which the entire universe from the very first moment of its existence had been orchestrated, fine-tuned" (pp. 7–8).

Ok, this quote is really deep and difficult to understand…What does "orchestrated" mean? Does this orchestra require a composer, a conductor and a concertmaster? How does Hebrews 11:10 relate to this? How does this Hebrew passage define God?

What does "fine-tuned" mean?

Was it fine-tuned for man to exist?

Who did the fine-tuning?

How about this quote?

Albert Einstein, the great physicist and Nobel Prize winner, saw awesome intelligence revealed in the existence of natural law. He wrote that the scientist's "religious feeling takes the form of a rapturous amazement at the harmony of natural law, which reveals an intelligence of such superiority that, compared with it, all the systematic thinking and acting of human beings is an utterly insignificant reflection" (Einstein: A Centenary Volume, ed. A. P. French, Harvard University Press, 1979, p. 305).

Some special thanks….

I want to thank the students of the Christian Campus house at Ball State University, where this study was first presented in the fall of 2017. Thank you: Andréa, Jessica, Madison, Clair, Ivory, Olivia, Alex, and Kyle. You guys are amazing and made this study fun to present and participate in.

The seven testimonies of God we are about to study show the glory and power of God! We experience these miracles every day, but at times with a hard heart (Mark 6:52) we cannot see or understand them. It takes eyes of faith to see God in these miracles. These seven witnesses will point you towards your Creator and reveal His power and love! These evidences are to be explored. In this exploration, make it fun. As my friend, Don Carpenter says, "OYM – Open Your Mind" -- Let this study open your mind!

A new concept has hit our society...**Evangelical Atheist**

> An **evangelical atheist** is an atheist who is not content merely with his own lack of faith but is also obsessed with censoring expressions of faith by others and attempting to sow disbelief in others around him.
>
> Examples of techniques used by evangelical atheists include:

- insisting that morality is independent of religion

- claiming that goodness is not achieved through attending religious services or reading the Bible

- insisting that it is hypocrisy for a sinner to attend church

- claiming to be smarter or superior than people who have faith

- using Darwinism as a weapon against Christianity

Retrieved from http://evangelicalatheist.com/2007/09/21/tyranny-of-the-majority/

Is this the society Christians live in today? This is one of the reasons why I wrote this study!

This study is designed to give seven testimonies of God. It will give evidences of God to help the Christian stand up to the secular, atheistic society. It will give tools to deal with the evangelical atheist. When confronted by this EA:

- Clarify the issue -- ask specifically what a person believes or does not believe. It is a valid approach to answer their questions to you with questions to them. Jesus often did this. (Mark 11:28-29)

- Defend with Biblical Christian thought (philosophy) and science.

- Challenge the EA to be intellectually honest.

What does Proverbs 26:26 teach?

What does Ephesians 5:11 teach? How do Christians do this to the EA?

This study has four elements and is based on the acrostic "sled". It will discuss:

Science: The word science comes from the Latin "scientia," meaning knowledge.

Retrieved from http://www.sciencemadesimple.com/science-definition.html

Most of us have been studying science since early elementary school. At times, this studying through the years has created careers and curiosity, which causes future investigations, and lifelong exploration.

I love science – psychological science. There are many Latin and Greek words used in science – that have English word links. This makes science even more fascinating to me. Look up the word "resist" in Greek. What is the English equivalency? This fascinates me…Look up the word "victory" in Greek. What is the English equivalency? Wow. Does this create a desire for more studying?

Science is a process of gaining knowledge that is ever growing. Science is often a group of theories with an ongoing process. Theories are an ongoing process…Science is a process not just a series of facts. Science is based on investigation.

One great irony of those who study science is that most people don't know what the word science means. Is that statement harsh? Ok, so define science?

Webster's New Collegiate Dictionary defines science as:

- "knowledge attained through study or practice,"

- "knowledge covering general truths of the operation of general laws, esp. as obtained and tested through scientific method [and] concerned with the physical world."

All of us need to become scientists – by knowledge attained through study. This Bible study will give you more knowledge about the testimonies of God. Using science, let me quote a real familiar passage, with a twist, "The fear of the Lord is the beginning of knowledge, but fools despise wisdom and discipline." Proverbs 1:7 -- So the twist, "Fear of the Lord is the beginning of science…"

Now try teaching that at University campuses today and see what happens. You will be ridiculed and made fun of. Don't be surprised (1 Peter 4:12-13). Stand firm. Make no apologies that you believe in God. No compromise in what you believe about there being a God -- and who God is and what he does -- like God as Creator and Sustainer!

Consider, impossible is not a scientific term! Impossible is God's reality. We live in that reality! (Matthew 19:26; Luke 1:37; Genesis 18:14)

Logical reasoning: Definition of logic: "A science that deals with the principles and criteria of validity of inference and demonstration: the science of the formal principles of reasoning."

Retrieved from https://www.merriam-webster.com/dictionary/logic

Logical thinking tends to be truth. Philosophical thinking tends to be reasoning…Reasoning can be sound or flawed. But what about logical reasoning?

Isn't it amazing that the word "biological" has the word logical in it? So, biology could be defined as the "logical reasons for life!"

This study is based on the idea that these seven testimonies are simple but when looked at are very complex. This simple but complex study requires some logic and reasoning.

Isaiah wrote about reasoning. Isaiah 1:18 states "and let us reason together…" I want to develop reasons for believing in God so that you can be reasonable when you reason with them! This is very close to 1 Peter 3:15 as stated previously.

The Hebrew word for "reason" is "yakach" (yaw-kahh'); a primitive root; to be right (i.e. correct); reciprocal, to argue; causatively, to decide, justify or convict: -appoint, argue, chasten, convince, correct (-ion), dispute, judge, maintain, plead, reason (together), rebuke, reprove (-r), surely, in any wise.

(Biblesoft's New Exhaustive Strong's Numbers and Concordance with Expanded Greek-Hebrew Dictionary. Copyright © 1994, 2003, 2006 Biblesoft, Inc. and International Bible Translators, Inc.)

Logic and reason fascinate me…Let me give you a problem

With a regular deck of playing cards of 52 – 26 with black suits and 26 red suits. You shuffle the deck seven times to get a good shuffled deck…you draw five cards. They are all red. What is the logical probability of it being a black card on the next draw? Is it one out of two or is it greater than that? Is the logical probability of a black card, 26/47 or 55.3%? It is 55.3%

Now let's look at an observation logically, (I love this quote),

From this picture, it is "reasonable" to believe that someone put this turtle on the fence post. Correct? Even though we did not see the person do it?

It is the same with our world and where it is in space and what it does in space. It is logical to believe in a Creator, even though we can't see him, except through the eyes of faith!

Consider this quote from CS Lewis, "Atheism turns out to be too simple. If the whole universe has no meaning, we should have never have found out that it has no meaning."

Evidence enlightenment: Evidence is defined as, 1. "Testimony and presentation of documents, records, objects, and other such items relating to the existence or non-existence of alleged or disputed facts into which a court enquires. 2. Methods and rules that guide and govern the establishment of a fact before a court, collectively called the law of evidence.

Retrieved from http://www.businessdictionary.com/definition/evidence.html

Enlightenment…means to open the mind, to put light in darkness.

Logical reasoning must be three things:

    Understandable

    Credible

    Intelligent

Consider this quote: "Aristotle suggests that a message's power to persuade is rooted in three factors: the logic of the argument (logos), the speaker's ability to project a trustworthy persona (ethos), and the speaker's ability to awaken the emotions of the audience (pathos)."

(Winsome Persuasion; Tim Muehlhoff and Richard Langer; InterVarsity Press; page 68)

Why must our logic, when expressed to others, be understandable? Why must our logic, when expressed to others, be credible? How would you describe credibility? The word credibility comes from Latin for "to believe."

Why must our logic, when expressed to others, be intelligent?

Evidence based theology and Christianity strengthens the answers to two distinct questions:

- What do you believe?

- How understandable and credible is the source?

Divine Design. Consider that if a simple instrument, such as a pencil, has a design and designer, how about a complex instrument, like the laptop computer I am writing with? What is more complex in our world, than our world, and everything in it?

How many steps and hours does it take to create a pencil from start to completion? How many steps and hours does it take to create a computer? What about a jet airplane -- how many hours and steps? The more complex something is, the more steps and hours to create it – correct? Look around, what is more complex, than our world and the universe it is in?

How about the human body, the most advanced machine on the planet? Consider:

- 18 days from conception, the heart beats.
- It has brain waves in 6 weeks.
- All the organs are functioning within 8 weeks.

But not all people see the human body or humanity as a testimony of God. Look at an interview with atheist Richard Dawkins and what he stated in an interview with Playboy:

PLAYBOY: You've described yourself as a "tooth fairy" agnostic. What is that?

DAWKINS: Rather than say he's an atheist, a friend of mine says, "I'm a tooth fairy agnostic," meaning he can't disprove God but thinks God is about as likely as the tooth fairy.

PLAYBOY: Let's turn to evolution, which many people misunderstand, such as believing we descend from apes.

DAWKINS: We are apes. We descend from extinct animals that would have been classified as apes. We are not descended from modern chimps or bonobos or gorillas. They've been evolving for exactly the same length of time as we have.

PLAYBOY: So what makes us human?

DAWKINS: We are a unique ape. We have language. Other animals have systems of communication that fall far short of that. They don't have the same ability to communicate complicated conditionals and what-ifs and talk about things that are not present. These are all unique manifestations of our evolved ape brain, which some evidence suggests came about through a rather limited number of mutations.

When it comes to the individuals Dawkins associates himself with, he admitted not having any "deeply religious friends." In addition to separating himself from those who believe in a higher power, Dawkins took a swipe at the intellectual capacity of those who embrace God.

"It's not that I shun them," he said of the religious. "It's that the circles I move in tend to be educated, intelligent circles, and there aren't any religious people among them that I know of."

Retrieved from http://www.theblaze.com/stories/atheist-richard-dawkins-tells-playboy-we-are-apes-evidence-for-jesus-existence-is-surprisingly-shaky-christ-dying-for-humanitys-sins-is-a-truly-disgusting-idea/

Abraham Vergehese once said, "Though I am fascinated by knowledge, I am even more fascinated by wisdom."   Does this describe some of Dawkin's statements? Which one of his statements made you laugh? What is the danger of being knowledgeable, but not wise?

Let me ask some questions of Richard Dawkins:

RD is my affectionate name for Richard:

> RD -- If I agree with you on evolution, am I enlightened?

> RD -- If I disagree with you, am I ignorant?

> RD -- Do we have a right to disagree with you?

> RD -- Do we have a right to debate you?

Quoting Hillary Clinton, sort of, "I'm sick and tired of people who say that if you debate and disagree with this administration, somehow you're not patriotic. We need to stand up and say we're Americans, and we have the right to debate and disagree with any administration."

> RD -- So, do I have a right to disagree and debate with you?

> RD -- I am not from the IVY league, am I intelligent?

> RD -- I am from the Midwest, not one of the coasts, do you struggle with me? Do you struggle with my intelligence?

> RD -- Do you think that you have a superior intelligence when it comes to how the world was formed? And what do you think about Bible believing Christians who believe that God created the world in 6 days and that Jesus resurrected in 3 days?

> RD -- Butterflies have four stages of development: egg, caterpillar, chrysalis and then a butterfly. So, evolution created all these stages? How?

> RD -- Let's think about the frog: a tiny egg hatches a tadpole. The tadpole has gills, so it can breathe in water, this tadpole eventually sprouts legs and loses its tail. And then it becomes an adult that can go on land and breathes air. And then the female mates and lays an egg…and the cycle beings again. What part of evolution created this?

RD – How many animals can breathe in both water and air?

RD -- Over the years, the length of time for the universe to evolve, has gone from millions of years to billions of years. Why is this?

At the closing of every session, it will state, what part of this study was:

- ✓ Science based
- ✓ Logic based
- ✓ Evidence Enlightenment
- ✓ Divine Design

Session 1

Let's start as children...

God revealed himself to children (Luke 10:21) and he wants us to be like children (Matthew 18:3).

"From the very beginning of his education, the child should experience the joy of discovery."
— Alfred North Whitehead

Acts 14:17 states, "Yet he has not left himself without testimony: He has shown kindness by giving you rain from heaven and crops in their seasons; he provides you with plenty of food and fills your hearts with joy."

The Greek phrase "without testimony" is the word **"amarturos"** (am-ar'-too-ros); unattested:

(Biblesoft's New Exhaustive Strong's Numbers and Concordance with Expanded Greek-Hebrew Dictionary. Copyright © 1994, 2003, 2006 Biblesoft, Inc. and International Bible Translators, Inc.)

We get the English word "amateur" from this Greek word. This study will take you from an amateur to a professional when it comes to explaining why you believe in God!

A Biblical truth... "No minds can conceive what God has prepared..." 1 Corinthians 2:9 Truth: There is knowledge (science) beyond our limited understanding. And the knowledge of science is constantly growing! God cannot be totally understood in the finite mind it takes faith. This study will strengthen your faith.

This Bible Study is based on seven evidential testimonies of God. These seven things are seen daily. From Acts 14:17, there are seven powerful testimonies of God: rain, heaven, crops in their seasons, food, hearts, and joy.

Every person who has ever lived has seen these seven pieces of evidence! Some believe, some don't. So believing is a choice. Faith is a human choice. Faith does not mean understanding. I will not be able to understand everything about these seven testimonies, but I have faith that God created all of them!

This verse seems very simple, that even a child could understand it. What did Jesus state in Luke 10:21 about who God reveals himself through? Maybe that is why the Holy Spirit directed Paul to speak these seven testimonies. This study is based on the idea of "simple -- but when studied -- it really is complex".

I can teach these seven testimonies to my four-year-old granddaughter, but I can go really deep with this passage and teach it to adults. This Acts 14:17 is really an amazing passage. It is a simple and straightforward passage. Albert Einstein would love this passage. He stated, "If you can't explain it to a 6-year-old, you don't understand it yourself.". Albert also stated, "It is enough if one tries merely to comprehend a little of this mystery every day. Never lose a holy curiosity. "

What a great statement "holy curiosity". Hopefully, this is what this study causes. Consider this quote, "If you're sincerely seeking God, God will make His existence evident to you." (William Lane Craig) Is this quote true? Is it true for everyone?

Ken Ham stated, "Evolutionists may claim that they 'follow the evidence where it leads,' but they have a bias and an interpretation of the evidence (just like biblical creationists). Our starting points determine how we build a worldview within which we interpret the evidence of the present in relation to the past."

Let's begin with a basic philosophy: One's interpretations will be influenced by one's presuppositions. So, if you presuppose there is no God, then your interpretation of the evidence is that there is no God! This is what is fascinating. We look at the same evidences but come to different conclusions. This must be because we start with different presuppositions! Our presuppositions are by choice; so, our belief in God is by choice! Our choice! A choice we all have to give an account for!

This Acts 14:17 verse does not use big theological words like "propitiation". (Try defining that one and use it in a sentence – I can't). This Acts passage uses very small words. C. S. Lewis would love this passage. He said, "Don't use words too big for the subject." Leonardo da Vinci said, "Simplicity is the ultimate sophistication."

Jesus made a great statement about God and who he reveals to, "At that time Jesus, full of joy through the Holy Spirit, said, 'I praise you, Father, Lord of heaven and earth, because you have hidden these things from the wise and learned, and revealed them to little children. Yes, Father, for this was your good pleasure.'" Luke 10:21

Jesus also said in Matthew 18:3, "I tell you the truth, unless you change and become like little children, you will never enter the kingdom of heaven."

Well, this Acts 14:17 passage is simplicity, but it contains a lot of depth when we dig into what it teaches. Paul wrote about people looking at the surface of things (2 Corinthians 10:7). I think he is telling people to go deeper into a topic. That is what this study will do.

Woody Guthrie said, "Any fool can make something complicated. It takes a genius to make it simple." This study is going to be the opposite of this quote, it is going to take the simple and show how really complex it is.

This Bible Study will address these seven testimonies of God and help you to defend why you believe in God. We are told by Peter to always be prepared to give an answer (1 Peter 3:15). This study will prepare you to give an answer, seven of them, to why you believe in God.

You will be questioned on what you believe. At times, you don't answer the question, you question the asker. You question them to clarify the issue. You can ask them specifically what a person believes or does not believe. This is where you begin…Challenge your listeners to be intellectually and scientifically honest about what they see in creation that blows their minds.

Consider this sad statistic…

70% of Christian College students lose their faith in College. Bombarded by beliefs, they cannot defend their faith and core beliefs. That is why I wrote this study…

You can find your own faith on Campus, which is a great reward; or you can be in a faith desert and your faith will dry up. Why are students on campuses losing their faith? They need to heed Paul's advice found in 2 Timothy 1:13, "Hold fast the form of sound words, which thou hast heard of me, in faith and love which is in Christ Jesus." KJV. Paul told Timothy to "hold on to the sound teachings – don't let go of it."…So when we are told things that don't align with scripture, we need to tell the teacher to "hold on" Which means to wait a minute, stop…let's clarify…

Consider this headline…"Liberal professors outnumber conservatives nearly 12 to 1, study finds"

Retrieved from https://www.washingtontimes.com/news/2016/oct/6/liberal-professors-outnumber-conservatives-12-1/

Wow, what is fair about that? If Christian students are not prepared for the assault on their faith is it is like an amateur fighting a professional. This is not a fair fight. So, in this study, I am going to level the playing field. This study is designed to be a help, a tool to minimize the threat or risk assessment of your faith. It is designed to give courage and strength to face this threat and risk head on! When we believe in God and creation is this declaring war on or with the secular culture? Are we in the minority? Consider:

> Belief in God drops below 90% among younger Americans, liberals, those living in the East, those with postgraduate educations, and political independents. However, belief in God is nearly universal among Republicans and conservatives and, to a slightly lesser degree, in the South.
>
> While some lament the secularization of America, these same individuals may be encouraged by Gallup's finding that only 7 percent of the nation doesn't believe in God's existence. Earlier this month, we reported on an Oxford study that claims belief in God is ingrained in our human nature.

Retrieved from http://www.theblaze.com/stories/92-of-americans-still-believe-in-god-but-youths-easterners-and-libs-arent-as-likely-to/

Consider these passages about Christians and the culture:

Matthew 28:15

>What story did the soldiers tell?
>
>Is this story being told today?
>
>What does this story sound like today?
>
>Is it that God does not exist? That Jesus is not real? That Jesus did not resurrect?
>
>What happens to the naïve in faith, when they hear this repeatedly?
>
>What does Luke 22:31-32 teach about the goal of this storyline?
>
>Are they like sheep among the wolves? (Matthew 10:16)?
>
>Are Christians prepared for the fight with the wolves?
>
>Are the wolves winning? Who are the wolves on college campuses? In society?
>
>How do the sheep get strengthened in their faith and win against the wolves?

Consider this William F. Buckley statement, "Liberals claim to want to give a hearing to other views, but then are shock and offended to discover that there are other views."

>Is this America today? Where do you find these offended people? What topics offended people?

Proverbs 29:10

>Why are we hated?

Proverbs 29:27

>Who detests in this passage?
>
>Why are they detested?

Matthew 10:16-17

>What is the relationship with these animals?

Luke 22:36

>What did Jesus tell us to purchase?

2 Timothy 3:12

>What is the promise of Paul in this passage?

Galatians 4:16

>Why does truth make people enemies?

Consider this research statistic:

>Less than 10 percent of British people, and only 15 percent of Canadians believe in the Creationist view that God created humans in their present form, a survey has found.
>
>The Newman University/YouGov survey, released on Tuesday, noted that 71 percent of people in the U.K. and another 60 percent of respondents in Canada accept evolutionary or theistic evolutionary accounts of how species on Earth came to be.

Retrieved from http://www.christianpost.com/news/less-than-10-percent-brits-minority-canadians-back-creationist-view-reject-evolution-198312/

So, is George Herbert correct, "Where god builds a church, the Devil will build a chapel"? George Herbert's Outlandish Proverbs (1640) no. 674

So, people believe that we live on an incredibly lucky terrarium that is perfect to have life! Look at our planet it just hangs in space. Job 26:7 states, "He spreads out the northern [skies] over empty space; he suspends the earth over nothing."

Who is the "He" in this passage? It is God.

Is the earth suspended over nothing?

Consider:

Earth has a consistent rotation. What would happen if our rotation was faster on this planet? What would happen if our rotation was not consistent?

We have a livable, stable gravity. Consider me, a 200-pound plus man waking up on Jupiter tomorrow, weighing 500 pounds plus. I am not sure my bone structure could support it…

So, consider Peter's statement in 2 Peter 1:3, "His divine power has given us *everything we need for life* and godliness through our knowledge of him who called us by his own glory and goodness."

Look up these scriptures and what they teach about God and creation

    Psalm 8:3-4

        When David looked at the heavens, what did David ponder?

    Psalm 33:6

        How did God create the stars?

Isaiah 40:21-22

>What are the two words that begin with c that are written in this passage?

>What is a canopy?

Psalm 19:1-2

>What does "declare" mean?

>Do the heavens "speak"?

>What do the heavens display day and night?

Romans 1:19-20

>How does God have invisible qualities that can be clearly seen?

Job 26:7-14

>Look at the powerful phrases in this passage

>>He spreads

>>He suspends

>>He wraps

>>He covers

>>He marks

>>By his power

>>By his breath

Why do people doubt God's power? Is it because they recognize they have limited power? So, do people limit God's power, by our lack of power?

The truth is you cannot prove there is a God. And the atheist cannot prove there is no God. So, believing in God is a person's choice and it takes faith. You do not have to possess full understanding to have faith! I do not fully understand how my remote starter works on my car, but I still have faith when I use it. What does the Bible teach about faith? Start reading Hebrews 11:1, 6. These are two very powerful passages on faith!

There is enough evidence to believe in God, so decide…we all see the same things on this planet and universe, so it must be a choice to believe or not believe.

This Bible study is a simple apologetics study…Apologetics may be simply defined as the defense of Christian faith.

> The word "apologetics" derives from the Greek word apologia, which was originally used as a speech of defense or an answer given in reply.

Retrieved from https://bible.org/seriespage/2-what-apologetics

Apologetic is the ability to answer questions, hoping to win some to your point of view or to change their mind. The word "apologetics" Greek "apologia," meaning "a verbal defense." This word is found eight times in the New Testament. (Acts 22:1; 25:16; 1 Corinthians 9:3; 2 Corinthians 10:5-6; Philippians 1:7; 2 Timothy 4:16, and 1 Peter 3:15). This Peter passage is the most familiar, "...but sanctify Christ as Lord in your hearts, always being ready to make a defense to everyone who asks you to give an account for the hope that is in you, yet with gentleness and reverence,"

There are a lot of people who make assertions and assumptions about there not being a God…but can they defend their arguments? This study is designed to help you defend your beliefs about God! To do it in a gentle way (1 Peter 3:15).

So why do you believe in God? Three weak answers are:

"Because I do"

"Because my parents taught me"

"Because I was taught in Church"

These three answers are woefully insufficient as a defense of your faith.

Put as another question, where is your evidence for the God you believe in? This study will give some great, simple, everyday evidences. The study will show that some very simple things are actually very complex and revealing.

So why do people believe in evolution when, as a theory, it has a difficult time explaining:

    Atoms to Adam

    Molecules to man

    Non-lethal mutations to create life as we know it.

    Nothing created everything

A question to ponder…Is science contrary to faith? Or can studying science, strengthen a person's faith? It is my belief that science will strengthen a person's faith!

Consider these quotes:

"To an atheist, the universe is the most exquisite masterpiece ever constructed by nobody." - G. K. Chesterton

What does Ephesians 2:10 (from the New Living Translation) teach?

Is the Universe finely tuned?

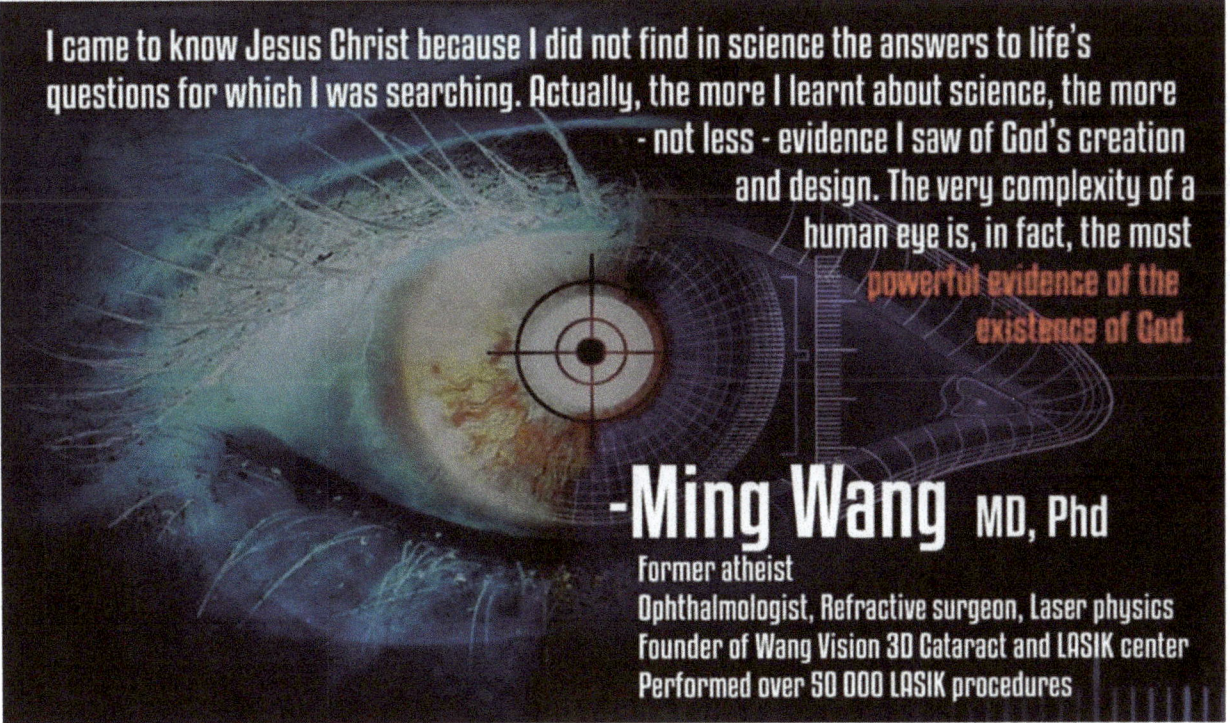

What was the powerful evidence that Dr. Wang saw?

What are "scientific observations"?

Consider, "A hypothesis is a limited explanation of a phenomenon; a scientific theory is an in-depth explanation of the observed phenomenon. A law is a statement about an observed phenomenon or a unifying concept, according to Kennesaw State University."

Retrieved from https://www.livescience.com/21457-what-is-a-law-in-science-definition-of-scientific-law....

What are the laws of physics and chemistry, this Doctor is referring to?

How does this relate to Job 38:33?

Consider this quote:

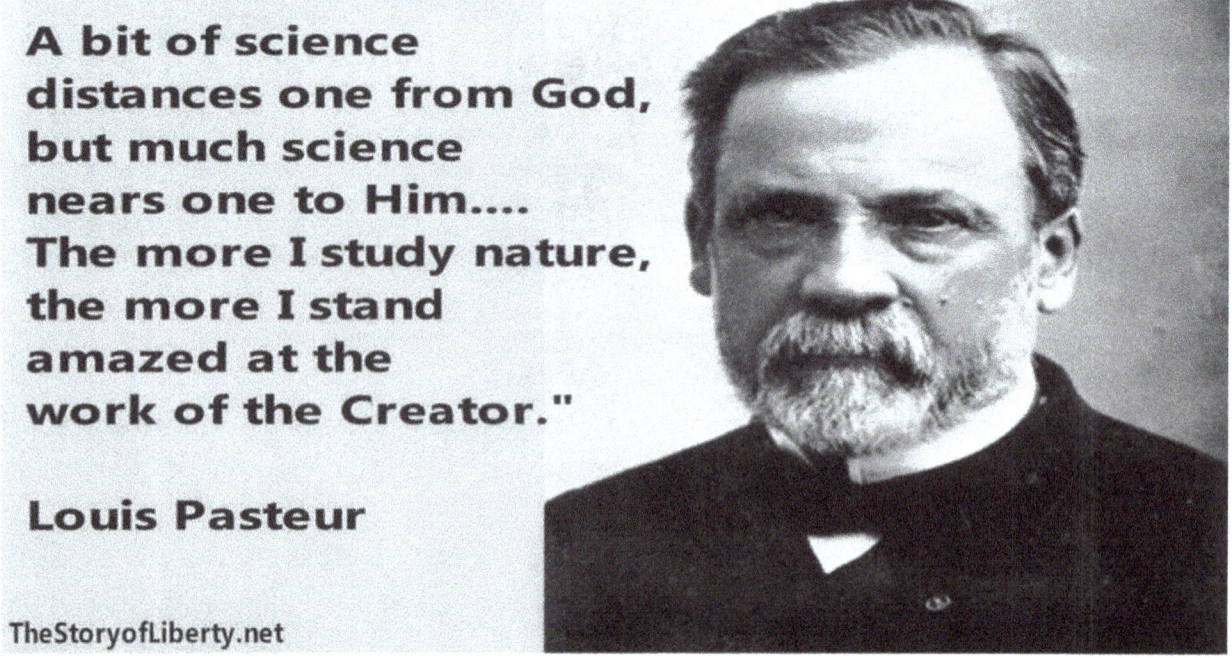

What made Louis Pasteur amazed?

Think about this quote, "I am an atheist, out and out. I don't have the evidence to prove that God doesn't exist, but I so strongly suspect he does not, I don't want to waste my time." Isaac Asimov

Isaac, I don't think that believing in God wastes your time, but actually enhances it.

And this quote, "The God of the Bible is also the God of the genome. God can be found in the cathedral or in the laboratory. By investigating God's majestic and awesome creation, science can actually be a means of worship." Francis Collins

The goal of this study -- think of the tennis shoe brand:

Know what you believe and that it is the truth John 8:32

Examine the truth Acts 17:11 Do you believe that truth should be examined and this should not be feared? Why would some people be afraid to examine truth?

Defend the truth Acts 17:2-4 This must be done with gentleness and respect (1 Peter 3:15).

Share the truth 1 Thessalonians 2:8 At times this sharing will be a conversation starter, at times it will be a conversation stopper. Don't be surprised and don't take it personally. I love what Luke 10:16 states, "He who listens to you listens to me; he who rejects you rejects me; but he who rejects me rejects him who sent me." Our goal is to speak the truth in love with gentleness and patience (Ephesians 4:15; Proverbs 25:15).

This Bible study series is based on one passage of the Bible...Acts 14:17 "Yet he has not left himself without testimony: He has shown kindness by giving you rain from heaven and crops in their seasons; he provides you with plenty of food and fills your hearts with joy."

These seven testimonies are significant for life to exist. The greatest testimony of God is life. Life of plants, animals, and human beings. Life is so fragile, and it requires an unexplainable balance to exist. One of my favorite descriptions of Jesus is "the Author of Life" (Acts 3:15). This fragile life and planet can be explained if there is an Author of life. What blows my mind is the atheist who believes that everything was created by nothing.

Consider these quotes…

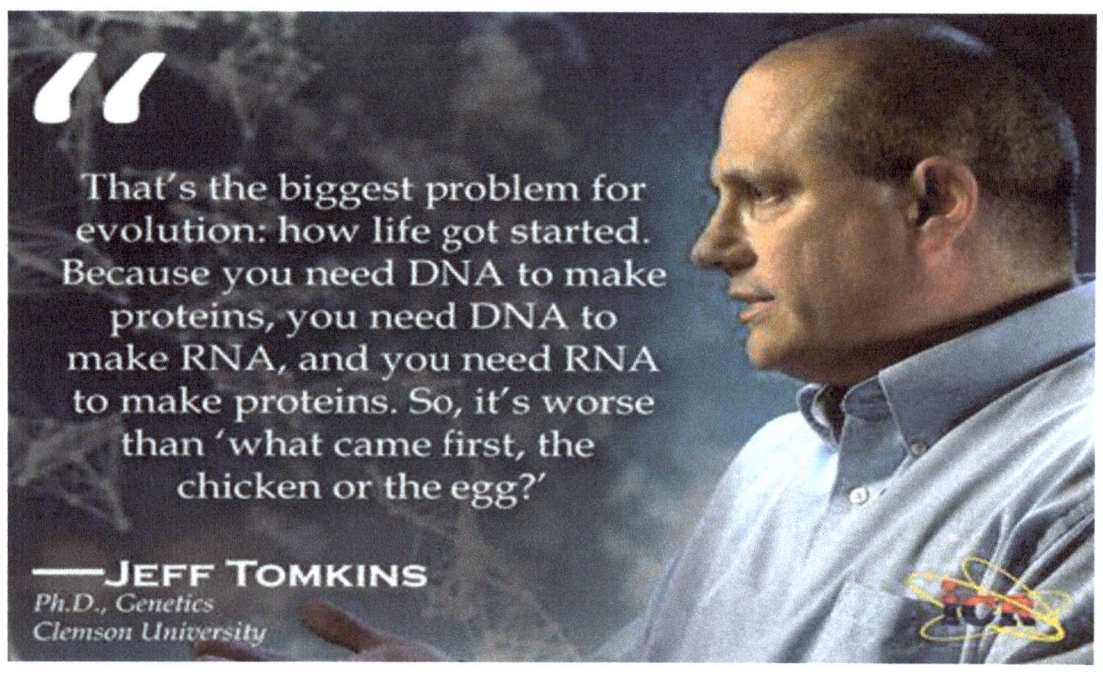

"God may exist, but I want more evidence and I've looked for it," He also notes that he can't bring himself to see the Bible as "the word of God." John Stossel

Retrieved from http://www.theblaze.com/news/2012/12/13/did-you-know-john-stossel-is-an-agnostic-watch-him-challenge-foxs-gretchen-carlson-on-religion

John, this study will give you the evidence -- observable evidence – knowledgeable, observable evidence. Consider, "Scientific observation is the central element of scientific method or process. The core skill of a scientist is to make observations.

Retrieved from https://explorable.com/scientific-observation

I love Jeff Foxworthy. What about this quote…

And what did Isaac Newton observe?

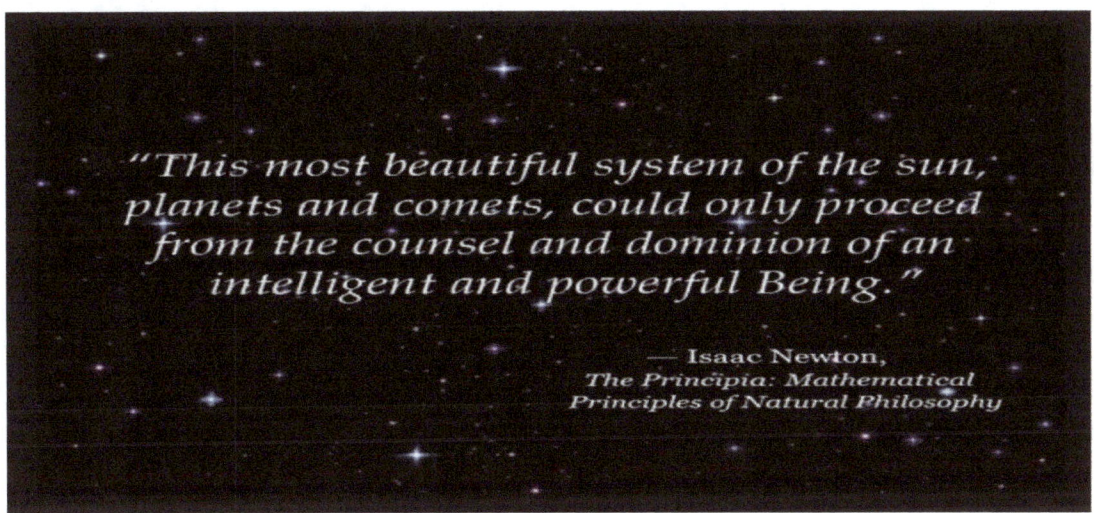

Is this picture below true when it comes to what is being taught about creation?

Consider what Blaise Pascal said, "There are only three types of people; those who have found God and serve him; those who have not found God and seek him, and those who live not seeking, or finding him. The first are rational and happy; the second unhappy and rational, and the third foolish and unhappy."

But a counterpoint is from Richard Dawkins, a famous atheist, who sees people who believe in creation as possessing "profound ignorance".

Retrieved from http://www.theblaze.com/news/2012/09/07/richard-dawkins-who-cares-about-creationists-their-deep-profound-ignorance-they-dont-know-anything

So, is ignorance the word they use when they cannot defend their beliefs about the issue? Will they then attack the individual? Richard, I am glad to be profoundly ignorant when it comes to me believing in God. Paul wrote in 1 Corinthians 1:27, "But God chose the foolish things of the world to shame the wise; God chose the weak things of the world to shame the strong."

And from Blaise again…"Men despise religion; they hate it and fear it is true. To remedy this, we must begin by showing that religion is not contrary to reason; that it is worthy of reverence and respect; then we must make it attractive, to make good men wish it were true; and then prove that it is true. Worthy of reverence because it really understands human nature. Attractive because it promises the true good." (Blaise Pascal Pensées pg. 187)

The philosopher Anthony Flew said: "If it is to be established that there is a God, then we have to have good grounds for believing that this is indeed so."

Retrieved from http://www.bbc.co.uk/religion/religions/atheism/beliefs/reasons_1.shtml

Oh, we have good grounds to believe in God, (pardon the pun), we live on it!

In closing, what part of this study was:

Science based

Logic based

Evidence Enlightenment

Divine Design

Session 2

The C's of life state there is a God

Let's look at the evidence that shouts there is a God. Let's start with one of the C's.

Constant Hebrews 13:8; Malachi 3:8; Colossians 1:17

How do you not believe in God when our universe moves at a constant velocity? To move at a constant velocity there has to be a constant power source. For there to be a constant power source there has to be a constant power supply. The power supply is that of a constant God. He holds everything together. Colossians 1:17.

A simple definition of God is power and energy…

Matter does not move itself. We are rotating on our axis 1017 miles an hour as we are going in orbit around the sun 64,000 miles an hour. This would take a lot of energy to do this continually. Albert Einstein came up with the theory of $E=mc^2$. This theory radically changed what we knew about how our Universe works. This theory says the Energy = Mass of an object times the speed of light (C) squared.

What is the mass of our planet?

"Although water covers 70 percent of the Earth's surface, water is actually a rare substance that represents just 0.05 percent of the Earth's total mass. Water has nevertheless played a crucial role in the emergence of life on Earth. Without water, the Earth would in all likelihood be a dead planet."

Retrieved from sciencenordic.com/earth-has-lost-quarter-its-water

Consider this statement, "Without water, the Earth would in all likelihood be a dead planet." Now let's not be PC, without water, the Earth would be a dead planet! There would be absolutely no life on this planet without water!

Two things fascinate me about our planet:

    It can sustain life.

    It has life.

These are two totally different things when you consider it. You should be totally amazed, and astonished and in awe of God and his power and majesty! (Habakkuk 3:2) Could our planet be able to sustain life, but not have it?

Earlier, I stated the earth revolves on its axis at a speed of 1017 miles an hour. This creates 24-hour days on earth. If this rotation was slowed to 10% of this speed, we would have longer days…10 times more sunshine and ten times more darkness. A day would be 240 hours. What would happen to life if this were the case? Plants would burn up during the long days with too long of heat exposure. At night the plants would die because of being exposed to too much darkness and the lower temperatures. Plants feed the animals. Animals would die. Animals feed humans, we would eventually die. Let's just keep the speed of the earth where it is right now.

Consistency of the creation

Science tells us that the next lunar eclipse will be April 8, 2024. And where I live, we will have "a total eclipse of the sun"…(Pardon the song)

Consider the seasons:

> Consistency of the order of the seasons
>
> Time of when the seasons begin

How about the consistency of Tides and Sunrise and Sunset?

I have a twin brother, Robert, (we are genetically consistent), who lives in Charleston, SC. He has taken us to a beach called Folly Beach. It is beautiful. I love the smell of the ocean, the sound at the beach and the smell of the beach. This beach also shows how consistent our world is. Consider this:

Folly Beach, Folly River bridge, Folly Island, South Carolina Tide Chart

February 2018

Day	High	Low	High	Low	High	Moon	Sunrise	Sunset
Thu 1		2:04 AM EST -1.2 ft	8:51 AM EST / 6.6 ft	2:41 PM EST -0.8 ft	9:18 PM EST / 5.7 ft		7:14 AM EST	5:52 PM EST
Fri 2		2:55 AM EST -1.1 ft	9:41 AM EST / 6.4 ft	3:29 PM EST -0.8 ft	10:09 PM EST / 5.7 ft		7:13 AM EST	5:53 PM EST
Sat 3		3:44 AM EST -0.9 ft	10:30 AM EST / 6.1 ft	4:15 PM EST -0.6 ft	10:59 PM EST / 5.6 ft		7:12 AM EST	5:54 PM EST
Sun 4		4:35 AM EST -0.6 ft	11:17 AM EST / 5.7 ft	5:02 PM EST -0.4 ft	11:50 PM EST / 5.4 ft		7:12 AM EST	5:55 PM EST
Mon 5		5:25 AM EST -0.2 ft	12:05 PM EST / 5.3 ft	5:50 PM EST -0.1 ft			7:11 AM EST	5:56 PM EST
Tue 6	12:41 AM EST / 5.2 ft	6:17 AM EST 0.1 ft	12:53 PM EST / 4.9 ft	6:39 PM EST 0.1 ft			7:10 AM EST	5:57 PM EST
Wed 7	1:34 AM EST / 5.1 ft	7:12 AM EST 0.4 ft	1:44 PM EST / 4.6 ft	7:31 PM EST 0.3 ft		Last Quarter	7:09 AM EST	5:58 PM EST
Thu 8	2:28 AM EST / 4.9 ft	8:10 AM EST 0.6 ft	2:37 PM EST / 4.4 ft	8:25 PM EST 0.4 ft			7:09 AM EST	5:59 PM EST

Day	High/Low	High/Low	High/Low	High/Low		Sunrise	Sunset
Fri 9	3:23 AM EST / 4.9 ft	9:07 AM EST / 0.7 ft	3:32 PM EST / 4.3 ft	9:20 PM EST / 0.4 ft		7:08 AM EST	6:00 PM EST
Sat 10	4:17 AM EST / 5.0 ft	10:03 AM EST / 0.6 ft	4:26 PM EST / 4.3 ft	10:14 PM EST / 0.3 ft		7:07 AM EST	6:00 PM EST
Sun 11	5:09 AM EST / 5.1 ft	10:55 AM EST / 0.5 ft	5:17 PM EST / 4.4 ft	11:04 PM EST / 0.2 ft		7:06 AM EST	6:01 PM EST
Mon 12	5:57 AM EST / 5.2 ft	11:42 AM EST / 0.3 ft	6:05 PM EST / 4.5 ft	11:50 PM EST / 0.0 ft		7:05 AM EST	6:02 PM EST
Tue 13	6:42 AM EST / 5.4 ft	12:27 PM EST / 0.2 ft	6:49 PM EST / 4.7 ft			7:04 AM EST	6:03 PM EST
Wed 14		12:33 AM EST / -0.1 ft	7:23 AM EST / 5.5 ft	1:09 PM EST / 0.0 ft	7:29 PM EST / 4.8 ft	7:03 AM EST	6:04 PM EST
Thu 15		1:15 AM EST / -0.2 ft	8:01 AM EST / 5.6 ft	1:48 PM EST / -0.1 ft	8:07 PM EST / 4.9 ft	New Moon	7:02 AM EST	6:05 PM EST
Fri 16		1:54 AM EST / -0.2 ft	8:37 AM EST / 5.5 ft	2:26 PM EST / -0.1 ft	8:43 PM EST / 5.0 ft	7:01 AM EST	6:06 PM EST
Sat 17		2:33 AM EST / -0.2 ft	9:11 AM EST / 5.5 ft	3:02 PM EST / -0.1 ft	9:20 PM EST / 5.1 ft	7:00 AM EST	6:07 PM EST
Sun 18		3:11 AM EST / -0.2 ft	9:46 AM EST / 5.4 ft	3:39 PM EST / -0.1 ft	9:57 PM EST / 5.2 ft	6:59 AM EST	6:07 PM EST
Mon 19		3:52 AM EST / -0.1 ft	10:21 AM EST / 5.2 ft	4:18 PM EST / -0.1 ft	10:39 PM EST / 5.3 ft	6:58 AM EST	6:08 PM EST
Tue 20		4:36 AM EST / 0.0 ft	11:02 AM EST / 5.1 ft	5:00 PM EST / -0.1 ft	11:27 PM EST / 5.4 ft	6:57 AM EST	6:09 PM EST
Wed 21		5:26 AM EST / 0.2 ft	11:49 AM EST / 4.9 ft	5:48 PM EST / -0.0 ft		6:56 AM EST	6:10 PM EST
Thu 22	12:22 AM EST / 5.4 ft	6:23 AM EST / 0.4 ft	12:46 PM EST / 4.7 ft	6:45 PM EST / 0.0 ft		6:55 AM EST	6:11 PM EST
Fri 23	1:25 AM EST / 5.4 ft	7:29 AM EST / 0.5 ft	1:52 PM EST / 4.6 ft	7:49 PM EST / 0.0 ft	First Quarter	6:54 AM EST	6:12 PM EST
Sat 24	2:34 AM EST / 5.5 ft	8:40 AM EST / 0.4 ft	3:03 PM EST / 4.6 ft	8:57 PM EST / -0.1 ft		6:53 AM EST	6:13 PM EST
Sun 25	3:43 AM EST / 5.6 ft	9:49 AM EST / 0.3 ft	4:14 PM EST / 4.8 ft	10:04 PM EST / -0.3 ft		6:52 AM EST	6:13 PM EST
Mon 26	4:50 AM EST / 5.9 ft	10:52 AM EST / 0.0 ft	5:20 PM EST / 5.0 ft	11:06 PM EST / -0.6 ft		6:51 AM EST	6:14 PM EST
Tue 27	5:52 AM EST / 6.1 ft	11:49 AM EST / -0.3 ft	6:21 PM EST / 5.4 ft			6:49 AM EST	6:15 PM EST
Wed 28		12:03 AM EST / -0.8 ft	6:49 AM EST / 6.3 ft	12:42 PM EST / -0.5 ft	7:16 PM EST / 5.7 ft	6:48 AM EST	6:16 PM EST

Retrieved from http://tides.mobilegeographics.com/calendar/month/1957.html

How in the world can this chart be accurate unless our world including the tides is consistent! Consistency is all around us….

> God's wisdom is revealed in His arrangement of sections and segments, as well as in the number of grains. Look at the consistency
>
> -Each watermelon has an even number of stripes on the rind.
> -Each orange has an even number of segments.
> -Each ear of corn has an even number of rows. An average ear of corn has 800 kernels, arranged in 16 rows.

-Each stalk of wheat has an even number of grains.
-Every bunch of bananas has on its lowest row an even number of bananas, and each row decreases by one, so that one row has an even number and the next row an odd number.
-All grains are found in even numbers on the stalks, and the Lord specified thirty fold, sixty fold, and a hundred fold all even numbers.
God has caused the flowers to blossom at certain specified times during the day. Linnaeus, the great botanist, once said that if he had a conservatory containing the right kind of soil, moisture and temperature, he could tell the time of day or night by the flowers that were open and those that were closed!

Retrieved from http://message.snopes.com/showthread.php?t=82452

Complex   (Psalm 139:14 NLT)

Our world is complex beyond comprehension. Let's look at one of the most amazing things God created -- the eye. Charles Darwin said about it, "To suppose that the eye . . . could have formed by natural selection, seems, I freely confess, absurd in the highest degree." (The Origin of Species by Means of Natural Selection or The Preservation of Favored Races in the Struggle for Life - Charles Darwin 1859, p. 217.)

Is the human eye "irreducibly complex"? What does "irreducibly complex mean? "Michael Behe gives the following definition of irreducible complexity: By irreducibly complex I mean a single system composed of several well-matched, interacting parts that contribute to the basic function, wherein the removal of any one of the parts causes the system to effectively cease functioning."

Retrieved from www.talkorigins.org/faqs/behe.html

Behold, the human eye.

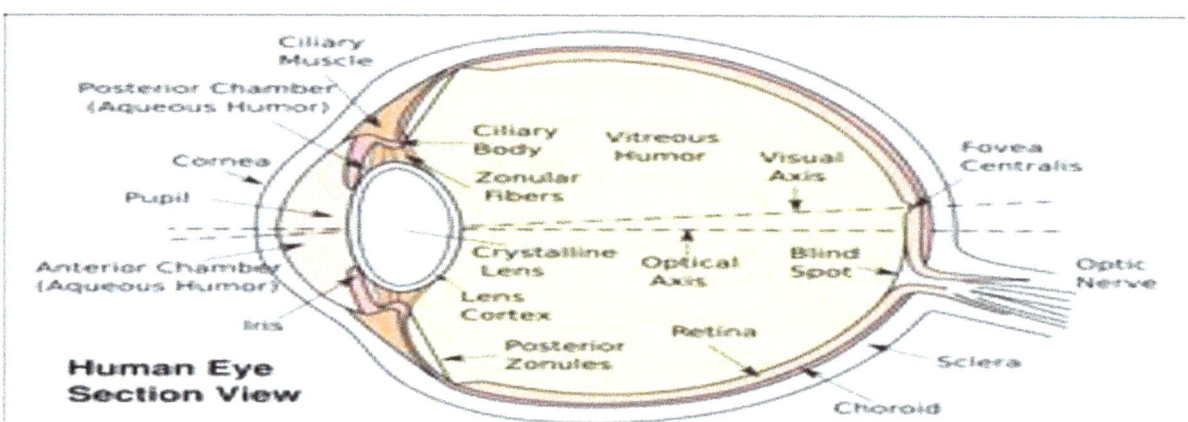

"There's a lot going on in there. The average human eye only weighs about 7 or 8 grams, but they are absolutely jam packed full of stuff. Chances are, you're the proud owner of two of these little beauties. Right now, they're busy using all of that intricate machinery to refract and focus light from your computer screen onto light sensitive rods and cones. From there, the light is being transduced into nerve signals, which are then being carried via your optic nerve into your visual cortex, where the raw information is getting filtered and patched together into something that you can make sense of."

Retrieved from https://skeptoid.com/blog/2013/12/24/is-the-human-eye-irreducibly-complex/

But there are people who believe in the evolution of the eye for the eye to be able to work properly…

Here's an abbreviated version of the leading model:

1. A mutation resulted in a single photoreceptor cell, which allowed the organism to respond to light and helped to calibrate circadian rhythms by detecting daylight.
2. Over successive generations, possessing multiple photoreceptors became the norm in the gene pool, because individuals with mutations encoding for an increased number of photoreceptors were better able to react to their surroundings. An arms race began, fueling the evolution of the new sensory organ.
3. Eventually, what was once just a single photoreceptor cell became a light-sensitive patch. At this point, the creature was still only able to distinguish light from dark.
4. A slight depression in the patch created a pit, for the first time allowing a limited ability to sense from which direction light or shadow was coming from.
5. The pit's opening gradually narrowed to create an aperture — like that of a pinhole camera — making vision sharper.
6. The aqueous humour formed. A colourless, gelatinous mass filling the chamber of the eye, it helped to maintain the shape of the eye and keep the light sensitive retina in place.
7. At the front, a transparent tissue with a concave curvature for refracting light formed. The addition of this simple lens drastically improved image fidelity.
8. A transparent layer evolved in front of the lens. This transparent layer, the cornea, further focused light, and also allowed for more blood vessels, better circulation, and larger eyes.
9. Behind the cornea, a circular ring formed, the iris, with a hole in its centre, the pupil. By constricting, the iris was able to control the amount of light that reached the retina through the pupil.
10. Separation of these two layers allowed another gelatinous mass to form, the aqueous humor, which further increased refractive power.

Retrieved from https://skeptoid.com/blog/2013/12/24/is-the-human-eye-irreducibly-complex/

Consider this information about the eye:

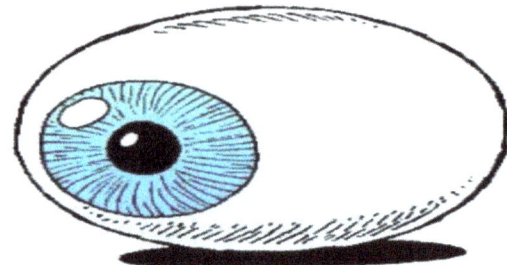

Forty subsystems? Working in harmony? All appearing at the same time? Does that scream "there has to be a Creator"?

Logical reasoning….would say yes…Does the eye require an intelligent design? I know this concept is not Politically correct…But is it logically correct? Defining intellect design,

"Intelligent design refers to a scientific research program as well as a community of scientists, philosophers and other scholars who seek evidence of design in nature. The theory of intelligent design holds that certain features of the universe and of living things are best explained by an intelligent cause, not an undirected process such as natural selection. Through the study and analysis of a system's components, a design theorist is able to determine whether various natural structures are the product of chance, natural law, intelligent design, or some combination thereof. Such research is conducted by observing the types of information produced when intelligent agents act. Scientists then seek to find objects which have those same types of informational properties which we commonly know come from intelligence. Intelligent design has applied these scientific methods to detect design in irreducibly complex biological structures, the complex and specified information content in DNA, the life-sustaining physical architecture of the universe, and the geologically rapid origin of biological diversity in the fossil record"

Retrieved from http://www.intelligentdesign.org/whatisid.php

I did ok with this definition until "during the Cambrian explosion approximately 530 million years ago." This website also goes on to state…

"Is intelligent design the same as creationism?

No. The theory of intelligent design is simply an effort to empirically detect whether the "apparent design" in nature acknowledged by virtually all biologists is genuine design (the product of an intelligent cause) or is simply the product of an undirected process such as natural selection acting on random variations. Creationism typically starts with a religious text and tries to see how the findings of science can be reconciled to it. Intelligent design starts with the empirical evidence of nature and seeks to ascertain what inferences can be drawn from that evidence. Unlike creationism, the scientific theory of intelligent design does not claim that modern biology can identify whether the intelligent cause detected through science is supernatural.

Honest critics of intelligent design acknowledge the difference between intelligent design and creationism. University of Wisconsin historian of science Ronald Numbers is critical of intelligent design, yet according to the Associated Press, he "agrees the creationist label is inaccurate when it comes to the ID [intelligent design] movement." Why, then, do some Darwinists keep trying to conflate intelligent design with creationism? According to Dr. Numbers, it is because they think such claims are "the easiest way to discredit intelligent design." In other words, the charge that intelligent design is "creationism" is a rhetorical strategy on the part of Darwinists who wish to delegitimize design theory without actually addressing the merits of its case."

I thought intelligent design would require an intelligent designer? Let me state several truths here, every design has to have a designer! So intelligent design requires intelligence! God is the only source of infinite intelligence. His wisdom, understanding, and intelligence are infinite, (therefore his wisdom, understanding, and intelligence cannot be fathomed by the finite mind of mankind. Mankind has intelligence because its Creator has intelligence. Artificial intelligence has to be created by real intelligence.

Look up the Youtube clip: "The Watchmaker"

Retrieved from https://www.youtube.com/watch?v=HwEhSsltU6k

I was taught in school that lightning struck a pond and created life…Eventually, this life crawled out of the water and it started to breathe air. Eventually, this air-breathing animal became a man. The most common thing on this planet that lightning hits daily…water…so we should see life being created all the time.

Consider, Eric Metaxes writes in a recent piece for the Wall Street Journal: "astrophysicists now know that the values of the four fundamental forces—gravity, the electromagnetic force, and the "strong" and "weak" nuclear forces—were determined less than one millionth of a second after the big bang. Alter any one value and the universe could not exist. For instance, if the ratio between the nuclear strong force and the electromagnetic force had been off by the tiniest fraction of the tiniest fraction—by even one part in 100,000,000,000,000,000—then no stars could have ever formed at all."

Retrieved from https://www.wsj.com/articles/eric-metaxas-science-increasingly-makes-the-case-for-god-1419544568

Can we even measure time in one millionth of a second?

Does that time frame blow your mind?

And how about the complexity of a cell…This next diagram is amazing…

THE COMPLEXITY OF ONE CELL SHOWS HOW SILLY THE THEORY OF EVOLUTION IS.

IF A PART OF THE CELL DID NOT WORK IT WOULD DIE, WHAT EVOLVED FIRST ?

What about the complexity of the creation? Consider how many functions the liver has…(this is one of the reasons why the theory of evolution falls apart).

Over 500 liver functions, including:

- Assimilating and storing fat-soluble vitamins
- Creating bile
- Filtering blood
- Metabolizing fats, proteins, and carbohydrates
- Metabolizing hormones, internally-produced wastes, and foreign chemicals
- Producing urea (a primary waste product, flushed from the body in urine)
- Purifying and clearing waste products, toxins, and drugs
- Regulating and secreting substances important to maintaining body functions and health
- Storing important nutrients (such as glycogen glucose), vitamins, and minerals
- Synthesizing blood proteins

Retrieved from http://www.puristat.com/livercleansing/liverfunction.aspx

Five hundred functions? Ok if the liver had five functions, I might believe in evolution. 50 functions, now that would really be a stretch for evolution. But 500 functions, evolution? Come on…Design – absolutely. Intelligent design – absolutely! How much intelligence would it take to create the liver?

Let's look at how **Creative** our world is:

One of the things I love about God is that He sets the rules of nature and then somewhere within that rule…He breaks it. Consider these breaks in creation:

"Antifreeze-Like Blood Lets Frogs Freeze and Thaw With Winter's Whims" (Thanks John and Vicki Hagerman for showing this to me.) This is nothing short of amazing! God rocks!

Retrieved from https://news.nationalgeographic.com/news/2007/02/070220-frog-antifreeze.html

Retrieved from https://answersingenesis.org/natural-selection/adaptation/the-secret-lives-of-frozen-frogs/

- Deer don't have gall bladders.

- Ants can walk vertically up and down a beam of wood. Trying to do that as a human.

- Snakes can climb up a wall of a barn.

- Almost all fish are cold-blooded (ectothermic). However, tuna and mackerel sharks are warm-blooded.

- The wombat poops square. This is really amazing when you think about it. God does this to make us question why?

- How about the lizard whose eyes move in two different directions?

- The hummingbird is the only bird that flies backward and hovers.

Why do I believe in God…because of the "beaver duck"…(Duck-billed platypus) Come on, you could not have created that. The duck-billed platypus is the only mammal that lays eggs. I can see God creating the front half of this animal and Jesus the back, and then they just put it together.

Complete If you were God what would you do differently on this earth, and with your body?

Read what 2 Peter 1:3-4 Consider what I highlighted….

"His divine power has given us everything we need for life and godliness through our knowledge of him who called us by his own glory and goodness. Through these he has given us his very great and precious promises, so that through them you may participate in the divine nature and escape the corruption in the world caused by evil desires."

Everything we need for life is found on this planet. The moon does not have everything we need for life. In fact, of all the planets in our solar system, Earth is the only planet that can sustain life. It also the only planet that has life! With all the planets in the universe, this blows my mind. And it is great evidence for my belief in God.

When I look at the evidence, I see the God of Creation. Another person sees the same evidence and does not see the God of Creation. It goes back to presuppositions. If I presupposed there is not a God, I will see the evidence through the filter that there is no God. It is the same for the person who believes. As a Christian, I see God's fingerprint on a large number of things.

In closing: What part of this study was

Science based

Logic based

Evidence Enlightenment

Divine Design

Session 3

The heavens

Where does rain come from? The heavens…I love what David wrote, "The heavens declare the glory of God; the skies proclaim the work of his hands." Psalm 19:1 For your knowledge base…The phrase "the heavens" occurs in the New International Version of the Bible 151 times. Proverbs 8:27 says that the heavens were set in place. Proverbs 8:29 says that seas have boundaries, that cannot be overstepped.

I love this picture…an Okinawa sunrise…Thanks, Amanda Rickey

And this sunset photo…Thanks, Jim Garringer

What do these skies proclaim?

From Genesis 1:8 what was called the sky? The expanse. Well, we now know the expanse is expanding.

I love the book of Isaiah. Look what it says in Isaiah 40:12, "Who has measured the waters in the hollow of his hand, or with the breadth of his hand marked off the heavens? Who has held the dust of the earth in a basket, or weighed the mountains on the scales and the hills in a balance?"

David wrote, "The heavens declare the glory of God; the skies proclaim the work of his hands. Day after day they pour forth speech; night after night they display knowledge." (Psalm 19:1-2) What is "knowledge"… "science"…so I can rewrite, "night after night they display science."

The heavens are more than just beautiful. Consider, "Over 98% of the charged particles from the Sun and from galactic cosmic rays that strike Earth's magnetosphere are deflected by it! The Van Allen Radiation Belts -- two doughnut shaped belts that surround the Earth -- trap the rest of the harmful particles, which bounce back and forth along magnetic field lines between Earth's north and south magnetic poles like beads on a wire."

Retrieved from http://www.spaceweathercenter.org/swop/Science_Briefs/Magnet/1.html

So are the heavens and these protective belts a testimony of God? Consider, "Our planet's magnetic field is believed to be generated deep down in the Earth's core."

Retrieved from http://www.physics.org/article-questions.asp?id=64

Does the size of stars and planets declare the glory of God? The Sun is very large compared to Earth. The Sun is 864,400 miles across. It is approximately 109 times the earth's diameter. The Sun weighs about 333,000 times as much as Earth. It is so large that about 1,300,000 planet Earths can fit inside of it.

> Are you surprised by the size of the sun?
>
> Does the size blow your mind?

But by comparison, the sun is not large. The largest star in the Milky Way galaxy is VY Canis Majoris. This is the big dog star. Its radius is 1,500 to 2,000 times larger than the Sun.

What do we know about the heavens? Let's begin with an Old Testament prophet…Isaiah "This is what the Lord says — your Redeemer, who formed you in the womb: I am the Lord, who has made all things, who alone stretched out the heavens, who spread out the earth by myself," Isaiah 44:24

> Are the heavens stretching out today? "In 1929 Edwin Hubble observed a very curious thing about galaxies. It appeared that most of the galaxies he observed were moving away from earth. Also, the farther away a galaxy appeared, the faster it seemed to be moving."

Retrieved from http://www.creationmoments.com/content/stretching-out-heavens

Let's look at two pictures that show the stretch of the heavens….

What two things does Deuteronomy 33:26 teach about God and the heavens and clouds?

What does Nahum 1:3 teach about clouds?

Is this a great visual?

Consider this picture of the Milky Way, which our solar system is in:

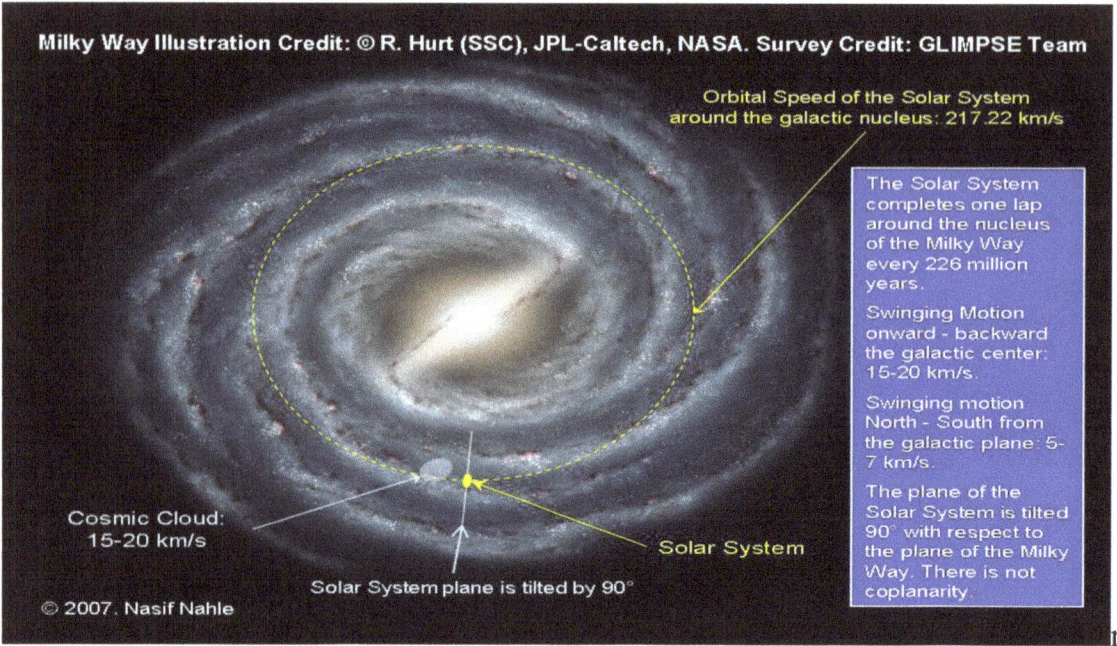

Consider this about our solar system:

> The Solar System is made up of all the planets that orbit our Sun. In addition to planets, the Solar System also consists of moons, comets, asteroids, minor planets, and dust and gas.
>
> It is true that there are only eight planets. However, the Solar System is made up of over 100 worlds that are every bit as fascinating. Some of these minor planets and moons are actually larger than the planet Mercury!
>
> Others, such as Io, have active volcanoes. Europa has a liquid water ocean, while Titan has lakes, rivers, and oceans of liquid Methane.

Retrieved from http://www.kidsastronomy.com/solar_system.htm

> …in 1999 the Hubble Space Telescope estimated that there were 125 billion galaxies in the universe, and recently with the new camera HST has observed 3,000 **visible** galaxies, which is twice as much as they observed before with the old camera. We're emphasizing "visible" because observations with radio telescopes, infrared cameras, x-ray cameras, etc. would detect other galaxies that are not detected by Hubble. As observations keep on going and astronomers explore more of our universe, the number of galaxies detected will increase.

Retrieved from http://imagine.gsfc.nasa.gov/docs/ask_astro/answers/021127a.html

Are those pictures not incredible?

Consider this about the heavens....

> A new study suggests that there are around 700 quintillion planets in the universe, but only one like Earth. It's a revelation that's both beautiful and terrifying at the same time.
>
> Astrophysicist Erik Zackrisson from Uppsala University in Sweden arrived at this staggering figure — a 7 followed by 20 zeros — with the aid of a computer model that simulated the universe's evolution following the Big Bang.
>
> Zackrisson's model combined information about known exoplanets with our understanding of the early universe and the laws of physics to recreate the past 13.8 billion years.

Retrieved from http://blogs.discovermagazine.com/d-brief/2016/02/22/earth-is-a-1-in-700-quintillion-kind-of-place/#.WYy4Lfl97IU

Genesis 2:1 states, "Thus the heavens and the earth were completed in all their vast array." The word vast...how vast is the universe? Jeremiah 31:37 states, "If only the heavens above can be measured..." Research shows it can, "The universe is at least 156 billion light-years wide."

Retrieved from www.cnn.com/2004/TECH/space/05/24/universe.wide/index.html

That is vast! Let's define the heavens: It is the Hebrews word, "shamayim" defined as "represents the realm in which the sun, moon, and stars are located." (from Vine's Expository Dictionary of Biblical Words, Copyright © 1985, Thomas Nelson Publishers.)

What does the Bible teach about the heavens? Isaiah has some great passages:

Read: Isaiah 34:4

>What did Isaiah state will happen with the heavens?
>
>How does this relate to Revelation 8:12?

From Isaiah 42:5

>What four ways does Isaiah describe God?
>
>What two things did God do with the heavens?
>
>What did God give to man?

From Isaiah 45:12

> What two things did God do with the heavens?
>
> What does it mean to marshal it?

Reading Jeremiah 10:12

> What three things did Jeremiah state that God possesses to create the heavens?
>
> Which of the three is the most difficult to comprehend?

Paul writes, "For by him all things were created: things in heaven and on earth, visible and invisible, whether thrones or powers or rulers or authorities; all things were created by him and for him." Colossians 1:16-17

David wrote that God breathed out the stars (Psalm 33:6). What a great visual verse. When I get to heaven I hope to see the video of creation. So how many stars are there?

What does Jeremiah 33:22 state about this? Are there more stars or grains of sand? Consider…

> If a grain of sand is 0.25 mm diameter, then you should be able to fit roughly 64 of them into a cubic mm (4 x 4 x 4 grains). There are 1000 cubic mm per cc (cubic centimeter, aka milliliter), so that gives 64000 grains per cc.
>
> A US cup is 236.6 cc, which means it would contain roughly 15 million grains of sand.
>
> If you go to a coarser sand with grains of 0.5mm, then there would be roughly 2 million grains per cup.

https://www.reddit.com/r/theydidthemath/comments/2r5gs5/request_how_many_grains_of_sand_are_in_a_cup_of/

Consider, these quotes….

"For many years scientists have studied our own solar system. But until the last few years, we knew of no other solar systems. This may seem surprising, as the Sun is one of about 200 billion stars (or perhaps more) just in the Milky Way galaxy alone."

Retrieved from https://spaceplace.nasa.gov/review/dr-marc-space/solar-systems-in-galaxy.html

Look at this amazing picture of the sun…

"So far, astronomers have found more than 500 solar systems and are discovering new ones every year. Given how many they have found in our own neighborhood of the Milky Way galaxy, scientists estimate that there may be tens of billions of solar systems in our galaxy, perhaps even as many as 100 billion."

Retrieved from https://spaceplace.nasa.gov/review/dr-marc-space/solar-systems-in-galaxy.html

"Astronomers estimate that the observable universe has more than 100 billion galaxies. Our own Milky Way is home to around 300 billion stars, but it's not representative of galaxies in general. The Milky Way is a titan compared to abundant but faint dwarf galaxies, and it in turn is dwarfed by rare giant elliptical galaxies, which can be 20 times more massive. By measuring the number and luminosity of observable galaxies, astronomers put current estimates of the total stellar population at roughly 70 billion trillion (7×10^{22})."

Retrieved from http://www.skyandtelescope.com/astronomy-resources/how-many-stars-are-there/

70 billion trillion now that number is vast…Genesis 2:1 I cannot even comprehend that number…Today is March 14 – Pi day…I cannot even comprehend pi… Consider, "The record for finding consecutive numbers, from 3.14 onward to the final digit, is held by Fabrice Bellard, who announced in January that he had calculated pi to 2.7 trillion digits."

Retrieved from www.bbc.com/news/technology-11313194

Ok, my mind is officially blown. Let's go back to our universe. So there is an observable universe, that means that is also an unobservable universe. This unobservable universe is huge. The Bible teaches that God stretched out the heavens (Job 9:8; Psalm 104:2; Isaiah 40:22; 42:5; 44:24; 45:12; 48:13; 51:13; Jeremiah 10:12; 51:15; Zechariah 12:1). Boy did He stretch it out. The span of the heavens is measured in light years.

Does "vastly infinite" describe the heavens? Can a human understand infinite? The human mind is finite, so it is logical to believe that the infinite cannot be defined by the finite! If the heavens are infinite and the mind cannot understand the infinite, we cannot understand the heavens.

Consider, "The speed of light in a vacuum is 186,282 miles per second (299,792 kilometers per second), and in theory nothing can travel faster than light. In miles per hour, light speed is, well, a lot: about 670,616,629 mph. If you could travel at the speed of light, you could go around the Earth 7.5 times in one second."

Retrieved from htttps://www.space.com/15830-light-speed.html

If we traveled at the speed of light or went into warp speed (I have seen Star Trek), I believe that our bodies would blow up because of the increased mass and the amount of G forces on our bodies. But let's say we can travel at the speed of light. So, if I traveled from Earth to Mars -- it is about 33.9 million miles. It would take about three minutes of travel at the speed of light. The earth to the moon would be like a second.

Some very smart people struggle with God and creation. Don't forget it was God's good pleasure to reveal himself to children, not to those in Mensa. Let's look at Stephen Hawking and his belief system.

Stephen Hawking: God did not create Universe

> The Universe can create itself from nothing, says Prof Hawking
>
> There is no place for God in theories on the creation of the Universe, Professor Stephen Hawking has said.
>
> He had previously argued belief in a creator was not incompatible with science but in a new book, he concludes the Big Bang was an inevitable consequence of the laws of physics.
>
> The Grand Design, part serialized in the Times, says there is no need to invoke God to set the Universe going.
>
> "Spontaneous creation is the reason there is something," he concluded.

Retrieved from http://www.bbc.co.uk/news/uk-11161493

Another quote from Stephen, "There is no heaven or afterlife for broken down computers; that is a fairy story for people afraid of the dark." Stephen Hawking

So Stephen, what caused the big bang?

So Stephen, who created the laws of physics?

What does spontaneous mean? Have we ever seen spontaneous creation created by nothing?

What did David write about the man who says there is no God? (Psalm 14:1; 53:1)

As I am finishing this study…Stephen died today (3/14/2018). He was 76 years old. He had dealt with ALS since he was about 21. Do you think his dealing with ALS was part of the issue why he did not believe in God?

Stephen said, "The greatest enemy of knowledge is not ignorance, it is the illusion of knowledge."

So, Stephen is now face to face with The God he did not believe in (his illusion of knowledge). This is a very scary situation. I do not possess the intellect of mind Stephen Hawking had. But, I would rather live here on earth with the unbelievable and unfathomable concept of Heaven (1 Corinthians 2:9), (and be found wrong), than to pass from this world and realize my concepts on life after death were wrong and shortsighted. Blaise Pascal called this The Wager.

The Wager is described by Pascal this way:

"God either exists or He doesn't. Based on the testimony, both general revelation (nature) and special revelation (Scriptures/Bible), it is safe to assume that God does in fact exist. It is abundantly fair to conceive, that there is at least 50 percent chance that the Christian Creator God does in fact exist. Therefore, since we stand to gain eternity, and thus infinity, the wise and safe choice is to live as though God does exist. If we are right, we gain everything, and lose nothing. If we are wrong, we lose nothing and gain nothing. Therefore, based on simple mathematics, only the fool would choose to live a Godless life. Let us see. Since you must choose, let us see which interests you least. You have nothing to lose. Let us estimate these two chances. If you gain, you gain all; if you lose, you lose nothing. Wager, then, without hesitation that He is."

Retrieved from https://www.york.ac.uk/depts/maths/histstat/pascal_wager.pdf

Questions about our solar system that will blow your mind:

    What makes all the planets stay in their orbit?

    What makes them move in their orbit?

    What force keeps all this going on in outer space?

    Why don't the orbits of the planets cross each other?

When did we learn the earth was round?

"Over 2,000 years ago, the Greek philosopher Aristotle had it all figured out. The fact that Earth is round has been common knowledge ever since.

In his book On the Heavens, he wrote: 'Again, our observations of the stars make it evident, not only that the Earth is circular, but also that it is a circle of no great size. For quite a small change of position to south or north causes a manifest alteration of the horizon.'"

Retrieved from http://www.bbc.com/earth/story/20160126-how-we-know-earth-is-round

This above statement, well it is not exactly correct. Isaiah 40:22 states, "He sits enthroned above the circle of the earth, and its people are like grasshoppers. He stretches out the heavens like a canopy, and spreads them out like a tent to live in."

Isaiah knew the earth was round in the mid to late 8th century BC. This was way before Aristotle.

"Around 330 BC, Aristotle provided observational evidence for the spherical Earth." (Lloyd, G.E.R. (1968). Aristotle: The Growth and Structure of His Thought. Cambridge Univ. Press, 162-164.)

Now a quote from whom my High School was named for:

"To look out at this kind of creation and not believe in God is to me impossible." (John Glenn) So. what did John Glenn observe that told him there a God? He had a view of the earth like none-other at the time. Was it his time in space that also helped him believe in God?

Consider this website -- "Six NASA Astronauts Describe the Moment in Space When 'Everything Changed'"

Retrieved from https://www.inverse.com/article/42902-nasa-astronauts-describe-overview-effect-everything-changed

Why did their point of view change?

In closing, what part of this study was:

Science based

Logic based

Evidence Enlightenment

Divine Design

Session 4

Rain – it is not all the same on all the planets

Let's look at one of the greatest evidences for a Creator God. Let's start with knowledge and reasoning.

Acts 14:17, seven powerful testimonies of God: rain, heaven, crops in their seasons, food and joy.

Rain....What does Matthew 5:45 teach about it? How is this a testimony about God?

What is another name for rain on earth? ....water.

Richard Bentley called water the "vital blood of the Earth" (I. B. Cohen (1958) Isaac Newton's Paper and Letters on Natural Philosophy (Cambridge: Cambridge University Press, pp. 381-382.

Consider what Leonardo Da Vinci stated, "Water is the driving force of all nature."

Truth: There is a delicate balance of many things on this planet for life to exist... Consider or reason..."If the pH of water is too high or too low, the aquatic organisms living within it will die. pH can also affect the solubility and toxicity of chemicals and heavy metals in the water. The majority of aquatic creatures prefer a pH range of 6.5-9.0, though some can live in water with pH levels outside of this range."

Retrieved from http://www.fondriest.com/environmental-measurements/parameters/water-quality/ph/

How would the death of aquatic organisms affect us? On our planet life is based on a food chain. A food chain is defined as "A series of organisms each dependent on the next as a source of food."

Retrieved from https://en.oxforddictionaries.com/definition/food_chain

If an animal that is low on the chain dies, then animals that depend on that animal for food would die. Do humans depend on the food chain for their food?

Let's consider other planets in our solar system. On earth, it rains water but, on other planets in our solar system....

What about living on Saturn or Jupiter? It rains diamonds! I know they are a girl's best friend, but I bet when they fall from the sky, that would create a lot of damage.

Retrieved from http://nypost.com/2013/10/15/its-raining-diamonds-on-saturn-and-jupiter/

"Unlike Earth's clouds, which are made of water, Venus' clouds are made of sulfuric acid that formed when water in the atmosphere combines with sulfur dioxide."

Retrieved from https://www.mnn.com/earth-matters/space/stories/what-does-it-rain-in-places-other-than-earth

How dangerous is sulfuric acid? "This chemical is unique because it not only causes chemical burns, but also secondary thermal burns as a result of dehydration. This dangerous chemical is capable of corroding skin, paper, metals, and even stone in some cases. If sulfuric acid makes direct contact with the eyes, it can cause permanent blindness."

Retrieved from https://www.msdsonline.com/.../sulfuric-acid-safety-tips-sulfuric-acid-msds-information/

Some planets rain:

    Liquid methane

    Glass

    Rocks

Retrieved from https://www.mnn.com/earth-matters/space/stories/what-does-it-rain-in-places-other-than-earth

Methane is the main component in natural gas. So it is important to us here on earth.

So, we are "lucky" that on earth it rains water! You have to admit that planet earth, is the perfect terrarium to sustain, maintain, grow and produce life. Think about that for a moment…accident or design?

Job 26:8 states, "He wraps up the waters in his clouds, yet the clouds do not burst under their weight." Job recognized the weight of water. Water is amazing when you think about it. If one acre of land had one inch of rain on it …that would be 226,000 pounds of water.

(https://water.usgs.gov/edu/earthrain.html) So why and how do clouds float? A gallon of water weights over 8 lbs. Clouds should not float, but knowledge says they do.

And how about the speed of the falling rain. Rain falls at about 14-20 mph on this planet.

(Retrieved from http://www.sciencefocus.com/article/planet-earth/how-fast-does-rain-fall)

What would happen if it fell faster? I love the sound of rain on a metal roof. But a hard rain can beat things down – like crops (Proverbs 28:3).

Rain in an important condition on Earth that allows for life. For life on this planet there needs to be at least four things: Retrieved from https://www.thestudentroom.co.uk/revision/environmental.../conditions-for-life-on-earth

- Water.
- Temperature. Most of the planet is above 0°C, so water in organisms does not freeze. It has the right temperature range for life to exist.

We live in suitable temperatures…even when it was -4 where I live yesterday. If we lived on the nearest celestial body to earth -- we would die…Consider the "temperatures on the moon are very hot in the daytime, about 100 degrees C. At night, the lunar surface gets very cold, as cold as minus 173 degrees C. This wide variation is because Earth's moon has no atmosphere to hold in heat at night or prevent the surface from getting so hot during the day." FYI 100°C = 212°F. FYI -173°C = -279°F

Antarctica holds earth's record low temperature -128.6 degrees Fahrenheit and the hottest record on this planet was in El Azizia, a desert, in Libya, 136 degrees. That's a temperature range of 265 degrees.

Consider this diagram about the temperature zones on this planet:

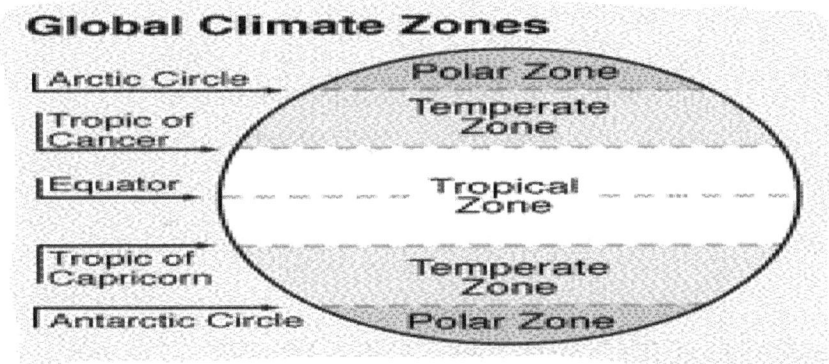

Retrieved from http://csc.gallaudet.edu/soarhigh/whyseasons.html

- Gases. The appropriate mix of gases are needed such as CO_2 for photosynthesis, oxygen for respiration and nitrogen for protein synthesis.

What keeps oxygen on this planet? Is there an airlock that keeps it on the earth?

Consider this statement about oxygen and what it states about how it "developed" on earth:

> Up until 2.45 billion years ago, there was almost no oxygen in the atmosphere. Then, cyanobacteria—the first known creatures to conduct photosynthesis—began to flourish. They released so much oxygen that it eventually became the second most common gas in our atmosphere. Ultimately, we have these tiny little creatures to thank for the oxygen we breathe today.

Retrieved from https://www.science.org.au/curious/space-time/goldilocks-planet

Are creatures capable of photosynthesis? I thought plants could do that!

Another name for cyanobacteria is blue-green algae. I don't think it flourishes in the atmosphere but in the oceans! I am sure earth gets a lot of its oxygen from algae, from the oceans and water.

> Scientists agree that there's oxygen from ocean plants in every breath we take. Most of this oxygen comes from tiny ocean plants – called phytoplankton – that live near the water's surface and drift with the currents. Like all plants, they photosynthesize – that is, they use sunlight and carbon dioxide to make food. A byproduct of photosynthesis is oxygen.
>
> Scientists believe that phytoplankton contribute between 50 to 85 percent of the oxygen in Earth's atmosphere.

Retrieved from http://earthsky.org/earth/how-much-do-oceans-add-to-worlds-oxygen

How important is oxygen to humans?

> In the human body, the oxygen is absorbed by the blood stream in the lungs, being then transported to the cells where an elaborated change process takes place.
>
> Oxygen plays a vital role in the breathing processes and in the metabolism of the living organisms.
>
> Probably, the only living cells that do not need oxygen are some anaerobic bacteria that obtain energy from other metabolic processes.

Retrieved from http://www.oxygen-review.com/human-body.html

But oxygen is more important just for respiration (which we do automatically). "Illness is the result of improper removal of toxins from the body. Oxygen is the vital factor which assists the body in removing toxins." Ed McCabe

Water has oxygen…Water is amazing…Almost every living thing needs water and oxygen. And it just happens to be found on this planet in abundance….

The last condition for there to be life on earth is:

- Light and solar radiation.

Let's go deeper into water…There are two amazing principles of water, buoyancy and thermal dynamics, that are amazing.

Water can float things. This is called buoyancy. Definition of buoyancy:

1a: the tendency of a body to float or to rise when submerged in a fluid

b chemistry: the power of a fluid to exert an upward force on a body placed in it

Retrieved from https://www.merriam-webster.com/dictionary/buoyancy

America would not have been discovered without buoyancy. (Buoyancy is known as Archimedes' Principle). Consider, the "Archimedes' principle, physical law of buoyancy, discovered by the ancient Greek mathematician and inventor Archimedes, stating that any body completely or partially submerged in a fluid (gas or liquid) at rest is acted upon by an upward, or buoyant, force the magnitude of which is equal to the weight of the fluid displaced by the body."

Retrieved from https://www.britannica.com/science/Archimedes-principle

Buoyancy is the opposite of gravity…Gravity is a downward force and buoyancy is an upward force. Don't forget that explorers got here by boats that floated. Salt water has greater buoyancy…than fresh water.

The economy of the world would be greatly hindered without buoyancy. Getting goods to the markets and ports would have been almost impossible. There are a lot of goods transported to markets by water.

Consider this water fact…The volume of water in the Amazon river is greater than the next eight largest rivers in the world combined.

Retrieved from https://www.deltacollege.edu/emp/pwall/documents/InterestingGeographyFacts.ppt

Consider why does a can of coke not float -- but a can of diet coke does? It is because of the sugar.

Thermodynamics is the study of heat. I love another physical law of water. It gets hot. Water being able to get hot and retain heat is the thermal principle of water….. I love hot showers. This is one of the gifts of God. I also love my morning coffee (with cream – not one of those fancy coffees like salted carmel etc.).

But there are limits to the heating capacity of water…

> It is always said that a person should be thankful for all the little things in life. But what about the really big things that have a dramatic effect on our lives. When was the last time you sat down and thought about what your life would be like if water did not have such a high specific heat capacity?
>
> Lucky for me, you, and our fish in the pond, water does indeed have a very high specific heat capacity. The specific heat of water is the amount of heat needed to raise its temperature a certain amount. One of water's most significant properties is that it takes a lot of heat to it to make it get hot. Precisely, water has to absorb 4.184 Joules of heat for the temperature of one gram of water to increase 1 degree celsius (°C). For comparison sake, it only takes 0.385 Joules of heat to raise 1 gram of copper 1°C.
>
> If you leave a bucket of water outside in the sun in summer it will certainly get hot, but not hot enough to boil an egg. But, if you walk barefoot on the black asphalt of a street here in Atlanta, Georgia in August, you'll burn your feet. Dropping an egg on the metal of my car hood on an August day will produce a fried egg. Metals have a much lower specific heat capacity than water. If you've ever held onto a needle and put the other end in a flame you know how fast the needle gets hot, and how fast the heat is moved through the length of the needle. Not so with water.

Retrieved from https://water.usgs.gov/edu/heat-capacity.html

Consider this about metal and melting:

"Most steel has other metals added to tune its properties, like strength, corrosion resistance, or ease of fabrication. Steel is just the element iron that has been processed to control the amount of carbon. Iron, out of the ground, melts at around 1510 degrees C (2750°F). Steel often melts at around 1370 degrees C (2500°F)."

Retrieved from https://education.jlab.org/qa/meltingpoint_01.html

> What would happen to life if water got that hot before it evaporated?
>
> Would people be injured in the shower?

Does the water testimony so far convince you that there is a God who designed water; and that the principles of water are God designed for life to be maintained?

Are rain and water miracles? Acts 2:22; John 14:11.

What does Genesis 2:5-6 teach about water on the earth before it rained?

What does it mean that streams came from the earth? "Groundwater is one of our most valuable resource—even though you probably never see it or even realize it is there. As you may have read, most of the void spaces in the rocks below the water table are filled with water. But rocks have different porosity and permeability characteristics, which means that water does not move around the same way in all rocks below ground."

Retrieved from https://water.usgs.gov/edu/earthgwaquifer.html

Look at what Psalm 104:24-28 teaches about rain…water….seas

Psalm 104:24

    What does this passage teach about God's creatures?

Psalm 104:25

    What are the three descriptions of the seas in this passage?

    What does beyond number mean?

We are learning more about the oceans all the time. Look at the words vast, spacious, and teeming. Wow. What are we learning more about the oceans? Are we learning more about the number of creatures in the ocean? Consider:

"There are 228,450 known species in the ocean — and as many as 2 million more that remain a total mystery.".

Retrieved from www.businessinsider.com/r-oceans-yield-1500-new-creatures-many-others-lurk-unknow...

Consider…"Most Earth species 'still unknown': Brazil expert"

SAO PAULO — "The vast majority of the Earth's estimated 13 million species are still unknown and to describe them all would take up to 2,000 years, according to a leading Brazilian scientist."

Retrieved from http://www.google.com/hostednews/afp/article/ALeqM5heHCs_uxY96rq5xSOkSMbB7ybnbw?docId=CNG.78c36afc5381b4873e84555a669f1477.891

I saw research that stated 94% of all life on earth is aquatic. That means that only 6 percent of life is on land. This same research stated we have only explored 5% of the oceans. My dad was in oceanographic when he was in the Navy -- the mapping of the oceans. In reality, scientists have mapped more of the moon than the oceans. Does this blow your mind?

Let me really blow your mind, "The longest mountain range in the world is under water. Called the Mid-Oceanic Ridge, this chain of mountains runs through the middle of the Atlantic Ocean and into the Indian and Pacific oceans. It runs more than 35,000 miles long, has peaks higher than those in the Alps and it comprises 23 percent of the Earth's total surface."

Retrieved from https://www.motherearthnews.com/nature-and-environment/nature/fun-surprising-facts-about-the-oceans

This ridge was not explored until 1973, four years after we landed on the moon!

Psalm 104:26

    What animals frolic in the oceans?

    Do dolphins?

    What about manatees?

    What about humans?

    How many times have you heard people use the phrase, "beach therapy"?

    What is beach therapy?

Psalm 104:27

    Where do the animals of the ocean get their food?

    Is there a food chain even in the ocean?

Psalm 104:28

Do the animals in the ocean gather to eat? On cruise ships, you will see this, and it is fascinating to watch.

Deuteronomy 33:13 teaches about deep waters in the oceans, and how the water below the earth also helps us live. The deepest part of the ocean is 36,200 feet. This is almost 7 miles. Put in perspective, the tallest mountain on land is Mount Everest at 29,029 feet tall. So, this mountain peak would be over 7000 feet below the water line.

Consider the Deepest Oceans & Seas:

    Pacific Ocean (35,837 ft)

    Atlantic Ocean (30,246 ft)

    Indian Ocean (24,460 ft)

    Southern Ocean (23,737 ft)

    Caribbean Sea (22,788 ft)

    Arctic Ocean (18,456 ft)

    South China Sea (16,456 ft)

Retrieved from https://www.worldatlas.com/aatlas/infopage/deepest.htm

But there are oceans we are unaware of. Consider this headline. "Massive 'ocean' discovered towards Earth's core"

Retrieved from https://www.newscientist.com/article/dn25723-massive-ocean-discovered-towards-earths-core/

How does this relate to Proverbs 8:28?

Things live in the depth of these oceans. Consider that "bacteria living in aphotic areas of the ocean are able to survive by chemosynthesis. They use energy derived from the oxidation of inorganic chemicals, such as sulfur released from deep hydrothermal vents, to produce their food."

Retrieved from www.dictionary.com/browse/chemosynthesis

Aphotic is where light does not go…Consider….

> Sunlight entering the water may travel about 1,000 meters (3,280 feet) into the ocean under the right conditions, but there is rarely any significant light beyond 200 meters (656 feet).
>
> The ocean is divided into three zones based on depth and light level. The upper 200 meters (656 feet) of the ocean is called the euphotic, or "sunlight," zone. This zone contains the vast majority of commercial fisheries and is home to many protected marine mammals and sea turtles.
>
> Only a small amount of light penetrates beyond this depth.
>
> The zone between 200 meters (656 feet) and 1,000 meters (3,280 feet) is usually referred to as the "twilight" zone, but is officially the dysphotic zone. In this zone, the intensity of light rapidly dissipates as depth increases. Such a miniscule amount of light penetrates beyond a depth of 200 meters that photosynthesis is no longer possible.
>
> The aphotic, or "midnight," zone exists in depths below 1,000 meters (3,280 feet). Sunlight does not penetrate to these depths and the zone is bathed in darkness.
>
> 'Photic' is a derivative of 'photon,' the word for a particle of light.

Retrieved from https://oceanservice.noaa.gov/facts/light_travel.html

When Moses wrote Deuteronomy 33:13, he did not even know anything about this or any of these oceans, but God did.

Did David understand about water? Psalm 77:19 What word did David use to describe the water? Is this word true? Where do you see the power of water?

What did David state in Psalm 65:5?

What did David state in Psalm 65:7?

I love the beautiful oceans and beaches. Are the oceans and beaches a miracle? They sure enhance life. We see them all the time, and probably take them for granted. I love taking cruises for vacation. When you are in the middle of the ocean and all you see is water, it is amazing.

Look at this picture…

This is an amazing masterpiece. The colors, the lighting, and the water are all amazing. I can see God doing this with a wonderful paint brush and an artistic mind.

Back to rain…What do these following passages teach about rain?

Jeremiah 5:24

    What should rain create for mankind?

    What does it mean to fear God?

    Does it mean respect God and hold him in ultimate honor?

Deuteronomy 11:14-15

    Who sends the rain?

    What does sends mean?

Job 5:10

    What does "bestows" mean?

    From Psalm 84:11; 133:3 what does God bestow?

Job 28:26

    What does decree mean?

Job 36:27

> Does this verse speak about evaporation?

Job 38:28

> What a great question from this passage.

In closing, what part of this study was:

Science based

Logic based

Evidence Enlightenment

Divine Design

Session 5

Other amazing water principles…

Water is found in three forms on this earth. Water as a solid, liquid and gas are all important to life. Solid water may be dangerous to life…Hail can be very destructive…Consider, the heaviest hailstone exceeded 1 Kg. (a little over 2 lbs.). This hail killed 92 people on 04/14/1986 in Gapalganj, Bangladesh.

Retrieved from www.guinnessworldrecords.com/world-records/heaviest-hailstones/

"The largest officially recognized hailstone on record to have been 'captured' in the U.S. was that which fell near Vivian, South Dakota last summer (2010) on July 23rd. It measured 8.0" in diameter, 18 ½" in circumference, and weighed in at 1.9375 pounds."

Retrieved from https://www.wunderground.com/blog/weatherhistorian/worlds-largest-hailstones.html

Consider "The costliest storm appears to be that of April 10, 2001 which cut a swath along the I-70 corridor from eastern Kansas to southwestern Illinois and pounded the St. Louis area. Property damage was in excess of $2.4 billion in 2010 dollars. The hailstorm that struck the Dallas/Ft. Worth, Texas metro area on May 5, 1995 also caused an estimated $2 billion in damage (adjusted to current dollars). The only other $1 billion dollar hailstorm on record was that which pummeled the Front Range of Colorado between Colorado Springs and Fort Collins on July 11, 1990 causing $1.6 billion damage in 2010 inflation-adjusted dollars."

Retrieved from https://www.wunderground.com/blog/weatherhistorian/worlds-largest-hailstones.html

"Hurricanes, floods and drought: Counting the cost for the US ag sector" By Aerin Einstein-Curtis

"Weather events from a series of cyclones to severe storms to inland floods to a crop freeze, drought and wildfire wreaked havoc for many sectors in the US last year including crop and livestock production; the disasters resulted in around $306.2bn in damages, estimates NOAA."

Retrieved from https://www.feednavigator.com/Article/2018/01/11/Hurricanes-floods-and-drought-Counting-the-cost-for-the-US-ag-sector

Is hail a testimony of God? Consider these passages….

Psalm 105:32-33

    Does lightning turn rain to hail?

    Is lightning caused when a warm front and a cold front collide?

Psalm 78:47-48

    What did hail cause from this passage?

Exodus 9:20-26

    From this passage, what was hail?

Job 38:22

    Where is the storehouse of hail?

Psalm 147:17

    What does God do with hail?

    What is the question of this passage? My answer to this question is "No!"

Psalm 148:8

    What does God's bidding? (There are five of them)

    What does "bidding" mean?

Isaiah 30:30

    What makes people hear God's majestic voice? (Five of them and three with water)

Isaiah 51:12-13 What can we do with God….Forget…that He is our Maker

    Do we think about God creating the foundation of the earth?

Jeremiah 10:10-12

    What are the three descriptions of God in vs. 10?

    What three things, found in vs. 12, did it take to create the earth?

Jeremiah 32:17

    What two things did it take to create the heavens and earth?

    Why is it difficult to comprehend the power of God?

    Why are the words "all powerful" and "impossible" not found in the same passage?

    Do you believe that there is nothing impossible with God?

    Do you live this belief out in your life?

Consider this majestic picture….Do you see the array of the sun?

Other amazing water principles…

- **Viscosity** -- the "thickness" of water allows for blood to flow through the capillaries.

    The human blood contains about 45% of erythrocytes and 54.3% of plasma by volume. The plasma contains about 92% water, while the erythrocytes, about 64% by weight.

    Blood is slightly less than 80% water.

    Dehydration occurs when water intake is insufficient to replace free water lost due to normal physiologic processes (like sweating, urination etc.). Hyponatremia is low sodium concentration in the blood. Usually, the Sodium and water concentrations in blood are regulated independently. Hyponatremia can be caused by intake of too much water, which reduces the sodium concentration.

References: The sodium, potassium, and water contents of red blood cells of healthy human adults by L J Beilin, G J Knight, A D Munro-Faure, and J Anderson, J Clin Invest. 1966 Nov; 45(11): 1817–1825.

What would happen if water had the same viscosity as corn syrup, cooking oil or honey…What would happen to our blood? I am not a doctor, but I believe that if blood were thicker, it would not flow properly though out the body. This would cause death. And if blood is too thin, this would also cause death.

So, we are dependent on water even for our blood….

- **The rainwater – vapor cycle** Solomon wrote in Ecclesiastes 1:7 "The rivers run into the sea but the sea is never full, and the water returns again to the rivers, and flows again to the sea." (Living Bible)

Elihu understood this principle…Job 36:27-30 NIV.

    What are the two "d" words found in vs.27?

    Which of these "d" words is most amazing?

    Did Elihu realize this vapor cycle principle before human science did? How?

    What does Jeremiah 10:13 teach about the clouds?

    What rises to the heavens to make clouds?

Consider these two diagrams…

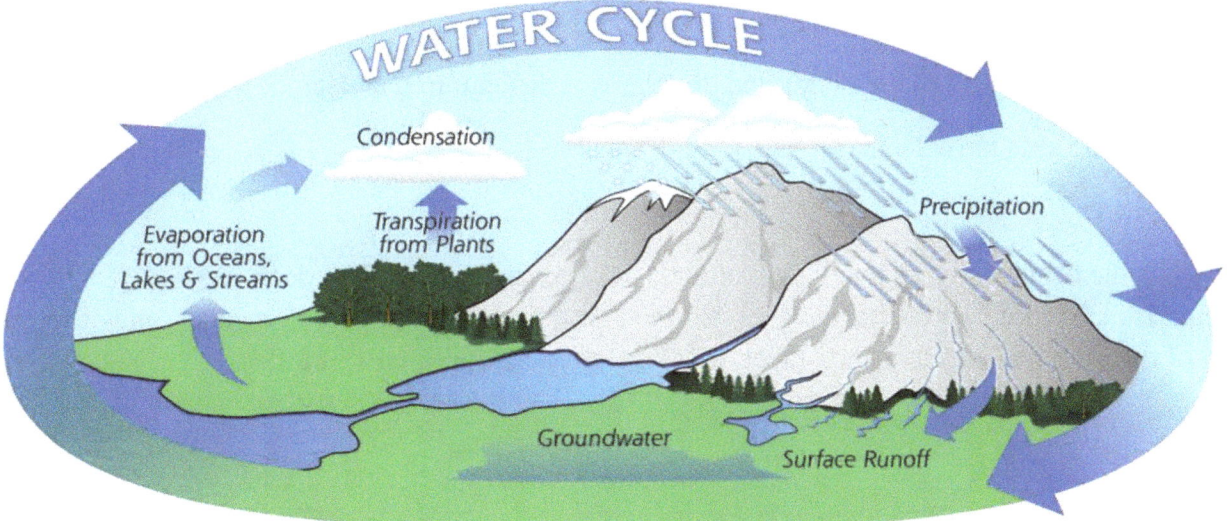

Retrieved from https://pmm.nasa.gov/education/water-cycle

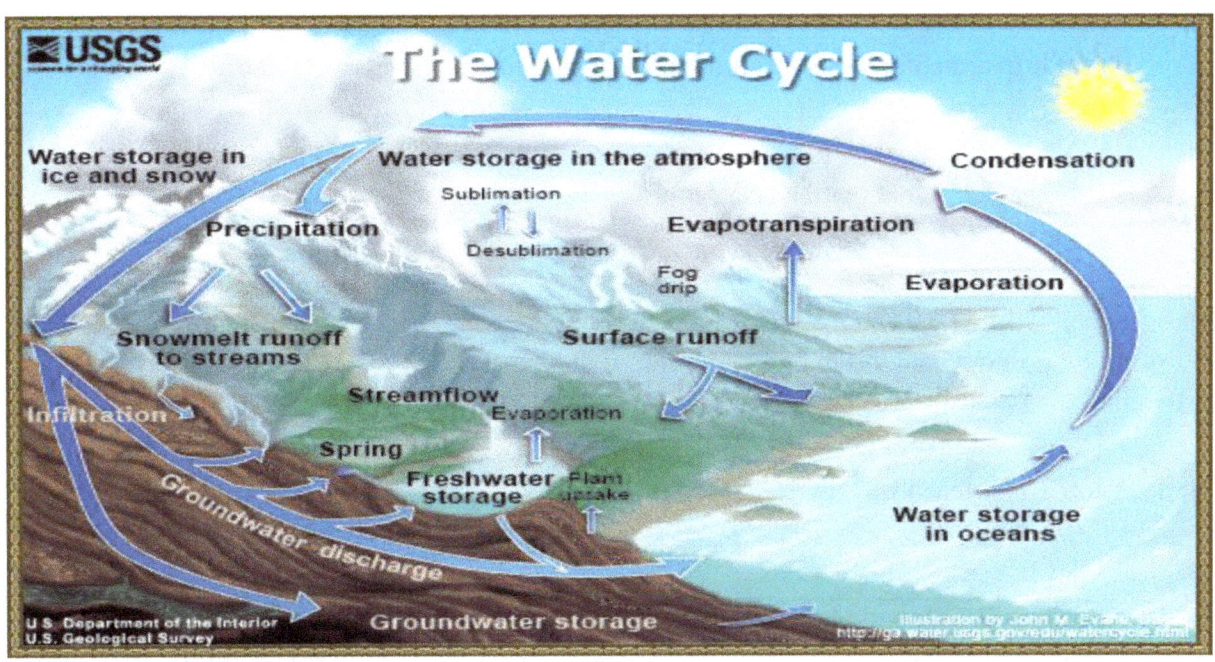

Retrieved from
https://www.google.com/search?q=USGS+water+cycle+diagram&tbm=isch&source=iu&ictx=1&fir=10mvwSrkaDY7WM%253A%252CjaP2yl-SycDsOM%252C_&usg=__f_Z6ANbTbLj83Y0UEZARzus_t3I%3D&sa=X&ved=0ahUKEwjPnceX3YfYAhWjzIMKHdI2CBkQ9QEIKTAA#imgrc=10mvwSrkaDY7WM:

What do clouds do in Job 36:28?

    Does our planet get abundant rain?

When you think about clouds and thunder is it difficult to understand? vs. 29

Do the seas have depths? Job 36:30; Psalm 148:8

Where is the deepest part of the ocean? It is the Marianna Trench. How deep is it? "By comparison, Mount Everest stands at 29,026 feet (8,848 m) above sea level, meaning the deepest part of the Mariana Trench is 7,044 feet (2,147 m) deeper than Everest is tall."

Retrieved from https://www.livescience.com/23387-mariana-trench.html

"However, Mauna Kea is an island, and if the distance from the bottom of the nearby Pacific Ocean floor to the peak of the island is measured, then Mauna Kea is 'taller' than Mount Everest. Mauna Kea is over 10,000 meters tall compared to 8,850 meters for Mount Everest - making it the 'world's tallest mountain.'"

Retrieved from https://geology.com/records/highest-mountain-in-the-world.shtml

What does Job 38:16 teach about the seas?

What does Psalm 148:7-10 teach about all these things praising God? Do these things praise God simply by doing what God intended them to do?

What does Job 36:33 teach?

Consider, "Studies have found that cows can conserve their body heat when they lie down, and since a drop in temperature is one of the hallmarks of a coming storm, it might imply that cows can sense the temperature drop and prepare for the rain and wind by lying down to retain their warmth. But, since we can't ask the cows if that's why they are lying down, it's just as possible that the cows are lying down just because they feel like lying down."

Retrieved from https://www.logicgoat.com/can-cows-tell-when-a-storm-is-coming/

Is Jacques Cousteau correct? "We forget that the water cycle and the life cycle are one."

Other amazing facets of water…

- **Capillary action and surface tension**

    Water has the highest surface tension among common liquids (mercury is higher). Surface tension is the ability of a substance to stick to itself (cohere). That is why water forms drops, and also why when you look at a glass of water, the water "rises" where it touches the glass (the "meniscus"). Plants are happy that water has a high surface tension because they use capillary action to draw water from the ground up through their roots and stems.

Environmental Science and Technology: Concepts and Applications by Frank R. Spellman page 411.

    The cohesive forces between liquid molecules are responsible for the phenomenon known as surface tension. The molecules at the surface do not have other like molecules on all sides of them and consequently they cohere more strongly to those directly associated with them on the surface. This forms a surface "film" which makes it more difficult to move an object through the surface than to move it when it is completely submersed.

    Surface tension is typically measured in dynes/cm, the force in dynes required to break a film of length 1 cm. Equivalently, it can be stated as surface energy in ergs per square centimeter. Water at 20°C has a surface tension of 72.8 dynes/cm compared to 22.3 for ethyl alcohol and 465 for mercury.

Retrieved from http://hyperphysics.phy-astr.gsu.edu/hbase/surten.html

One of the things I love about rain is lightning…I love lightning. I grew up near San Francisco and I never saw it until I moved to northern Indiana. One of my favorite passages on the power of God is Psalm 18:12, think of the William Tell Overture. My paraphrase, God holds the power of lightning in the palm of his hand. When I see lightning, I think of God.

Amazing facts about lightning. "The average lightning bolt measures about an inch wide and five miles long. But the longest bolt ever recorded occurred in the Dallas area, and crossed an impressive 118 miles. The temperature of lightning can reach around 50,000° F. The electricity in a single bolt can reach 200 million volts."

Retrieved from https://curiosity.com/topics/how-big-is-a-lightning-bolt/

Elihu understood lightning…Job 36:30, "See how he scatters his lightning about him, bathing the depths of the sea."

Let me blow your minds about lightning

"About 100 lightning bolts strike the Earth's surface every second. That's about 8 million per day and 3 billion each year."

Retrieved from https://learn.weatherstem.com/modules/learn/lessons/36/02.html

That number blows my mind…

What do these passages teach about lightning?

Psalm 77:18-19

    How does God's lightning light up the whole earth?

Psalm 97:4-6

Psalm 135:7; Matthew 24:27; Revelation 16:18

How important is lightning for life?

"When lightning slices through the atmosphere, it knocks electrons from the nitrogen atoms. The atoms are then free to combine with oxygen and hydrogen in the atmosphere forming nitrates. Rain carries this new compound to the earth enriching the soil with nitrates which are the building blocks of proteins."

Retrieved from www.dandydesigns.org/id22.html

How about what lightning does for the plants? It actually helps them grow!

Retrieved from http://www.daytondailynews.com/news/how-does-lightning-help-plants-and-flowers/ouBLyRRxVWvffWEGciES6N/

> This, as most other of the Atheists' Arguments, proceeds from a deep Ignorance of Natural Philosophy; for if there were but half the sea that now is, there would also be but half the Quantity of Vapours, and consequently we could have but half as many Rivers as now there are to supply all the dry land we have at present, and half as much more; for the quantity of Vapours which are raised, as well as to the heat which raised them. The Wise Creator therefore did so prudently order it, that the seas should be large enough to supply Vapours sufficient for all the land.

John Ray, 18th century British Naturalist (John Ray, The Wisdom of God Manifested in the Word of Creation, 1701; Michael Denton, Nature's Destiny, p. 73)

- **Top-down freezing of water**

What would happen if ice did not float?

This is great because ice floating on top of a body of water lets the rest of it stay liquid. If ice sank, whole oceans could freeze solid! And all forms of life in ponds, lakes, streams, rivers, seas, and oceans would die.

> The mere freezing of water is a miracle staggering in its significance. By all the rules of physical behavior ice should not float. Almost every substance, whether solid, liquid or gas, will shrink in volume as its temperature goes down. Water follows this rule precisely as a gas and, as a liquid, for 96 percent of the way down the temperature range to its freezing point. But at 39.2 degrees Fahrenheit something happens. As cooling continues, instead of shrinking, the water expands. The icy molecules seem to trap air molecules in their frosty structures, freezing into a solid at 32 degrees Fahrenheit, forming chunks of ice that float with about nine-tenths of the bulk submerged under the surrounding water.
>
> If it were not for this phenomenon—this wonder of floating ice—the world's seas, lakes and rivers would slowly freeze solid, depriving the earth of its much-needed water supply. But as it is, when winter comes, ice forms and floats on the surface of bodies of water, forming an insulating skin that protects the water beneath from further freezing and so safeguards the living things there.

Retrieved from http://www.blurtit.com/q670383.html

What does floating ice do?

Water gets into rocks, freezes and breaks them up. Water goes into the soil in winter and freezes and thaws repeatedly. This breaks up the soil -- making it easier for planting and plowing.

What does Acts 4:24 teach about water?

Consider…

> An estimated 50-80% of all life on earth is found under the ocean surface and the oceans contain 99% of the living space on the planet. Less than 10% of that space has been explored by humans. 85% of the area and 90% of the volume constitute the dark, cold environment we call the deep sea.
>
> "Currently, scientists have named and successfully classified around 1.5 million species. It is estimated that there are as little as 2 million to as many as 50 million more species that have not yet been found and/or have been incorrectly classified."
>
> According to World Register of Marine Species (WoRMS) there are currently at least 226,408 named marine species (9/24/2014).
>
> So, there are at least 226,408 marine species but there are most likely at least 750,000 marine species (50% of 1.5 million species) and possibly as many as 25 million marine species (50% of 50 million species).

Retrieved from http://marinebio.org/marinebio/facts/index.aspx

How does this relate to Revelation 10:6?

How much water is on the earth? "Recent estimates put the volume of the Earth's oceans at 1.332 cubic kilometers. This is equivalent to around 3.52×10^{20}, or 352 quintillion, gallons of water. As a note, this estimate was made using satellite data to obtain sea surface area, and an average ocean depth of 3.682 km."

Retrieved from https://www.quora.com/How-many-gallons-of-water-are-in-the-oceans-

Now that is a lot of water…What do you know about water?

Did you know this about WATER?

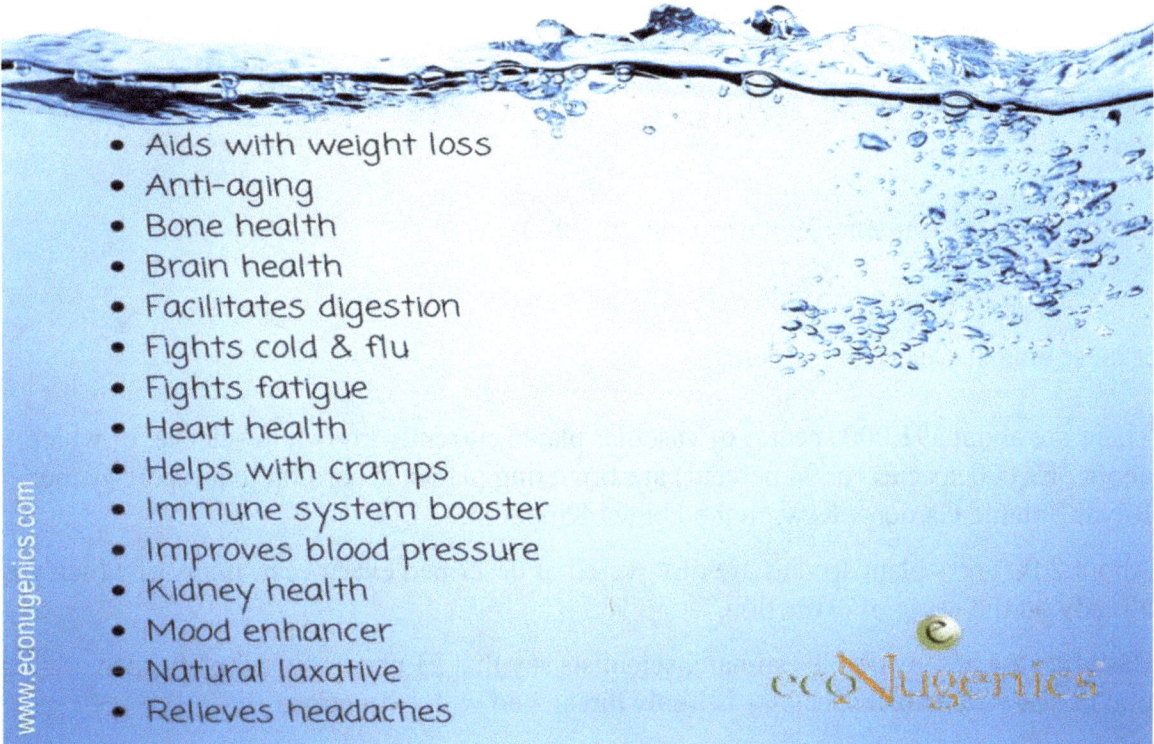

It is no doubt that water is a blessing from God. Rain is a blessing from God! What can God do with water?

Genesis 2:4-6, 10-14

>What did not happen before it rained?

>Where did God get water before it rained from the heavens?

>How did God water the Garden of Eden?

Genesis 8:1-2

>What did God do with rain?

Exodus 9:33-34

>What did God do through Moses?

Leviticus 26:4

> What happens because of rain in the seasons?

Deuteronomy 11:11

> What does the land do with rain?

What did God do in the Garden of Eden? (Genesis 2:8-9)

Consider these amazing facts about plants:

- There are about 391,000 species of vascular plants currently known to science, of which about 369,000 species (or 94 percent) are flowering plants, according to a report by the Royal Botanic Gardens, Kew, in the United Kingdom.
- About 2,000 new plant species are discovered or described every year, many of which are already on the verge of extinction.
- Based on the best available estimate, scientists say that 21 percent of all plant species – or one in every five plant species – is likely threatened with extinction.

Retrieved from https://news.mongabay.com/2016/05/many-plants-world-scientists-may-now-answer/

Consider these two quotes: "The world record for the fastest growing plant belongs to certain species of the 45 genera of bamboo, which have been found to grow at up to 91 cm (35 in) per day or at a rate of 0.00003 km/h (0.00002 mph)."

Retrieved from http://www.guinnessworldrecords.com/world-records/fastest-growing-plant/

"Bamboos are a group of woody perennial evergreen plants in the true grass family Poaceae. Some of its members are giants, forming by far the largest members of the grass family. There are 91 genera and about 1,000 species of bamboo. They are found in diverse climates, from cold mountains to hot tropical regions."

Retrieved from https://www.sciencedaily.com/terms/bamboo.htm

Deuteronomy 11:17: 28:24

> What did God do when he was angry?

Deuteronomy 28:12

    What did God do with rain from this passage?

    How does this relate to 1 Kings 8:35-36; 1 Kings 17:1; 1 Kings 18:1?

1 Samuel 12:18; (Jeremiah 2:19)

    What made the people stand in awe of Samuel?

    When you see these things, do you stand in awe?

2 Samuel 22:12-14

    What are the testimonies of God found in this passage?

Psalms 135:7

    What does God do with clouds and wind?

Psalms 147:8

    What are three things God does according to this passage?

    FYI: There are more than 12,000 species of grass.

What did Jesus do with water?

- He walked on it   Matthew 14:22-33
- He turned it into wine   John 2
- He knew where the fish were in the lake   Luke 5:4-6
- He calmed the storm   Mark 4:35-41

    What two things were the disciples afraid of in this storm encounter?

These four miracles show the power that God and Jesus have over nature (John 20:30-31). Stated again, God makes the natural laws and somewhere within the natural laws, He breaks them. God is not bound by natural law because he is Almighty and the creator of the natural law! He is not bound by the natural laws of physics, chemistry, time or space!

How could Jesus do this with water? In John 10:30, Jesus said he and God are one. Jesus is not bound by the natural laws because he created them (Colossians 1:16-17) and therefore he can break them! God is the lawgiver (Isaiah 33:22)!

All creation obeys Jesus and God! What did Paul write in Colossians 1:17? What does it mean He is before all things? What does it mean that he holds all things together? So, would things fall apart without God and Jesus holding things together?

Paul in Colossians 2:9-10 writes that all the fullness of God was in Jesus and that Jesus is the head over every power and authority.

- He used it as a conversation starting point with the woman at the well (John 4). This dialogue is amazing. We find in this passage the compassion of Jesus towards those who are considered the outcasts of society. He talks to her about living water (John 4:10, 11).

    The phrase "living water" is found in the NIV seven times. (Jeremiah 2:13; 17:13; Zechariah 14:8; John 4:10-11; 7:37-40; Revelation 7:17)

    The phrase "never thirst" is found two times (John 4:14; Revelation 7:16)

    Revelation 21:6 states that when God gives us this water it is without cost!

What else did Jesus do with water?

- He got baptized in it. Matthew 4

    Look at 1 Peter 3:18-22

    What is a good conscience before God?

    How important is this type of conscience?

    Peter mentioned Noah. With water, God destroyed the earth and its inhabitants, but He also saved Noah and his family.

In closing, what part of this study was:

Science based

Logic based

Evidence Enlightenment

Divine Design

Session 6

What Are the Elements in the Human Body?

The best in the universe ...

"Without a doubt, the most complex information-processing system in existence is the human body. If we take all human information processes together, i.e. conscious ones (language, information-controlled, deliberate voluntary movements) and unconscious ones (information-controlled functions of the organs, hormone system), this involves the processing of 1024 bits daily. This astronomically high figure is higher by a factor of 1,000,000 [i.e., is a million times greater] than the total human knowledge of 1018 bits stored in all the world's libraries."

Dr Werner Gitt, in Information: The Third Fundamental Quantity, (reprint from) Siemens Review, 56(6), November/December 1989.

If there was no water, there would be no human body. Consider:

Water is of major importance to all living things; in some organisms, up to 90% of their body weight comes from water. Up to **60%** of the human adult body is water. According to H.H. Mitchell, Journal of Biological Chemistry page 158, the brain and heart are composed of **73%** water, and the lungs are about 83% water.

Each day humans must consume a certain amount of water to survive. Of course, this varies according to age and gender, and also by where someone lives. Generally, an adult male needs about 3 liters per day while an adult female needs about 2.2 liters per day. Some of this water is gotten in food.

Water serves a number of essential functions to keep us all going:

- A vital nutrient to the life of every cell, acts first as a building material.
- It regulates our internal body temperature by sweating and respiration

- The carbohydrates and proteins that our bodies use as food are metabolized and transported by water in the bloodstream;
- It assists in flushing waste mainly through urination
- acts as a shock absorber for brain, spinal cord, and fetus
- forms saliva
- lubricates joints

According to Dr. Jeffrey Utz, Neuroscience, pediatrics, Allegheny University, different people have different percentages of their bodies made up of water. Babies have the most, being born at about 78%. By one year of age, that amount drops to about 65%. In adult men, about 60% of their bodies are water. However, fat tissue does not have as much water as lean tissue. In adult women, fat makes up more of the body than men, so they have about 55% of their bodies made of water.

Retrieved from https://water.usgs.gov/edu/propertyyou.html

What do the following two passages teach about human creation?

Psalm 139:13-16

    What words are amazing in this passage that describe the human body? Is the body an amazing feat of engineering?

Job 10:9-12

    What words are amazing in this passage that describe the human body?

What Are the elements in the human body? Most of the human body is made up of water, H_2O, with cells consisting of 65-90% water by weight. Therefore, it isn't surprising that most of a human body's mass is oxygen. Carbon, the basic unit for organic molecules, comes in second. 99% of the mass of the human body is made up of just six elements: oxygen, carbon, hydrogen, nitrogen, calcium, and phosphorus.

1. Oxygen (65%) We could not have water without oxygen! This begs the question…

How does air stay on Earth, but not escape off into space?

> The reason why air stays on Earth, but not in space is the same reason why a ball thrown in the air comes back down to Earth and does not go off into space: gravity. All gases that make up the atmosphere, like the ball, have mass, and therefore "fall" towards the Earth because of gravity. However, all molecules in the air have some energy which depends on the temperature. Hydrogen molecules, which are the lightest, often get enough energy to escape Earth's gravity and go off into space. Planets with stronger gravity, like Jupiter, can hold on to even the hydrogen in their atmosphere. Small planets or moons may not have enough gravity to hold on to any gases.

Retrieved from http://www.gk12.research.pdx.edu/question/how-does-air-stay-earth-not-space

2. Carbon (18%)
3. Hydrogen (10%)

What do oxygen and hydrogen form....Water!

4. Nitrogen (3%)
5. Calcium (1.5%)
6. Phosphorus (1.0%)
7. Potassium (0.35%)
8. Sulfur (0.25%)
9. Sodium (0.15%)
10. Magnesium (0.05%)
11. Copper, Zinc, Selenium, Molybdenum, Fluorine, Chlorine, Iodine, Manganese, Cobalt, Iron (0.70%)
12. Lithium, Strontium, Aluminum, Silicon, Lead, Vanadium, Arsenic, Bromine (trace amounts)

Reference: H. A. Harper, V. W. Rodwell, P. A. Mayes, *Review of Physiological Chemistry*, 16th ed., Lange Medical Publications, Los Altos, California 1977.

All these chemicals must be in the precise amount. Too little or too much and life does not exist…This has got to be done by intelligent design!

Logic says that the more complex and complicated something is, it requires more intelligence and ability to create it.

What are the four organic molecules found in living things?

All organisms need four types of organic molecules: nucleic acids, proteins, carbohydrates and lipids; life cannot exist if any of these molecules are missing.

Nucleic Acids. The nucleic acids are DNA and RNA, or deoxyribonucleic acid and ribonucleic acid, respectively. ...

Proteins. ...

Carbohydrates. ...

Lipids.

Retrieved from education.seattlepi.com/four-organic-molecules-found-living-things-5567.html

Are these part of our DNA code?

"That's how much information is stored in the DNA inside every human cell: the entire human genome. If you sort through the three billion letters that make up the human genome, you find some surprising things. Only about 1% of the three billion letters directly codes for proteins."

Retrieved from https://www.dnalc.org/resources/3d/09-how-much-dna-codes-for-protein.html

"Each single nucleotide has a compound called phosphate, (a compound is a combination of two or more elements) a sugar called deoxyribose and a compound called a base. The phosphate and sugars are the same in all DNA nucleotides, but the bases aren't. Thymine, adenine, guanine, and cytosine are the four DNA bases."

Retrieved from www.gwinnett.k12.ga.us/LilburnES/PromoteGA/biochemistry/DNA_makeup.html

Consider this quote….

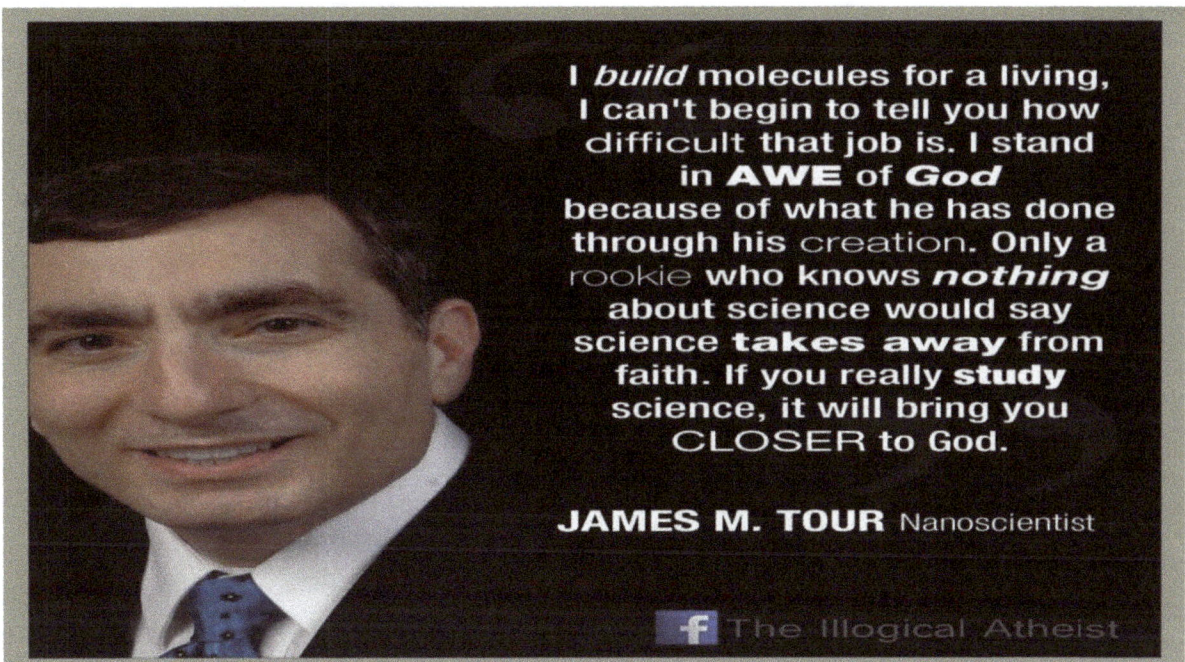

The body has many biological systems -- all of these systems require water to work! At least 60% of the adult body is made of water. Every living cell in the body needs it to keep functioning. These systems have several functions that have to work in coordination. These systems also have to work in coordination with each other. It is like a machine with multiple parts and gears. If one does not work in coordination with the others, the machine does not work.

The systems of the body are:

- The Circulatory System

- The Digestive System Our body can digest food. This is a testimony of God by itself. "Your body contains an enzyme called amylase, which breaks down carbohydrates in the food you eat into glucose, which your cells can use as energy."

Retrieved from http://education.seattlepi.com/four-organic-molecules-found-living-things-5567.html

- The Endocrine System "The endocrine system is the collection of glands that produce hormones that regulate metabolism, growth and development, tissue function, sexual function, reproduction, sleep, and mood, among other things."

Retrieved from https://www.livescience.com/26496-endocrine-system.html

- The Excretory System This one eliminates waste from the body.

- The Immune System

- The Integumentary System

    skin   hair   nails   glands

- The Reproductive System

- The Respiratory System

- The Muscular System

- The Nervous System

- The Skeletal System

These systems must operate in coordination. They are all interconnected. They all need each other! All these systems had to develop at the same time for life to exist! How would evolution explain all of these systems being developed at the same time, so there can be life?

They had to be created all at the same time and they must work in harmony. What would happen if all the systems of the body took millions of years to go on line? Like it took man 1 million years before he could digest food or eliminate waste! What would have happened if it took 1 million years after life existed before our reproductive system went on line?

With all of these systems, is the body frail? Is the body resilient?

Can the body adapt quickly? "In a harsh environment — it's snowing, say — you have 3 hours to survive without shelter. After 3 days, you need water or you'll perish. You can make it 3 weeks without food, though we promise you that won't be fun. Despite this possibly helpful rule, some people have survived 8 to 10 days without water."

Retrieved from https://www.livescience.com/32320-how-long-can-a-person-survive-without-water.html

Without water, how dangerous is dehydration to the body?

> "The combination of dehydration and overheating sends thousands of people to hospital emergency rooms each year, but diarrhea, excessive vomiting, and kidney failures of various sorts can also cause dehydration. A person can stay hydrated by drinking many different kinds of fluids in addition to water, with one exception. Drinking alcoholic beverages actually causes dehydration because ethanol depresses the level of the anti-diuretic hormone arginine vasopressin (AVP). As a result, urine volume increases such that more fluid is lost in urine than is gained by consuming the beverage."

Retrieved from https://www.scientificamerican.com/article/how-long-can-the-average/

In closing, what part of this study was:

Science based

Logic based

Evidence Enlightenment

Divine Design

Session 7

The four seasons (not the singing group)

How great is our God?

Consider these pictures….

The colors of the seasons, the beauty! Who could create colors except God?

Look at the variations of color. Doesn't this look like a painting by God? It is part of his masterpiece! Look at how the water is like a mirror and reflects the image…

Great is our God!!! Our Creator and Redeemer . . . and do we THINK about it?

What causes the seasons?

The seasons are caused by the tilt of the Earth's rotational axis away or toward the sun as it travels through its year-long path around the sun. The Earth has a tilt of 23.5 degrees relative to the "ecliptic plane" (the imaginary surface formed by it's almost-circular path around the sun). Nov 26, 2010

Retrieved from www.weatherquestions.com/What_causes_the_seasons.htm

"The moon ensures that Earth's tilt remains stable, so seasons won't ever vanish completely."

Retrieved from https://www.livescience.com/18972-earth-seasons-tilt.html

Consider these two pictures…

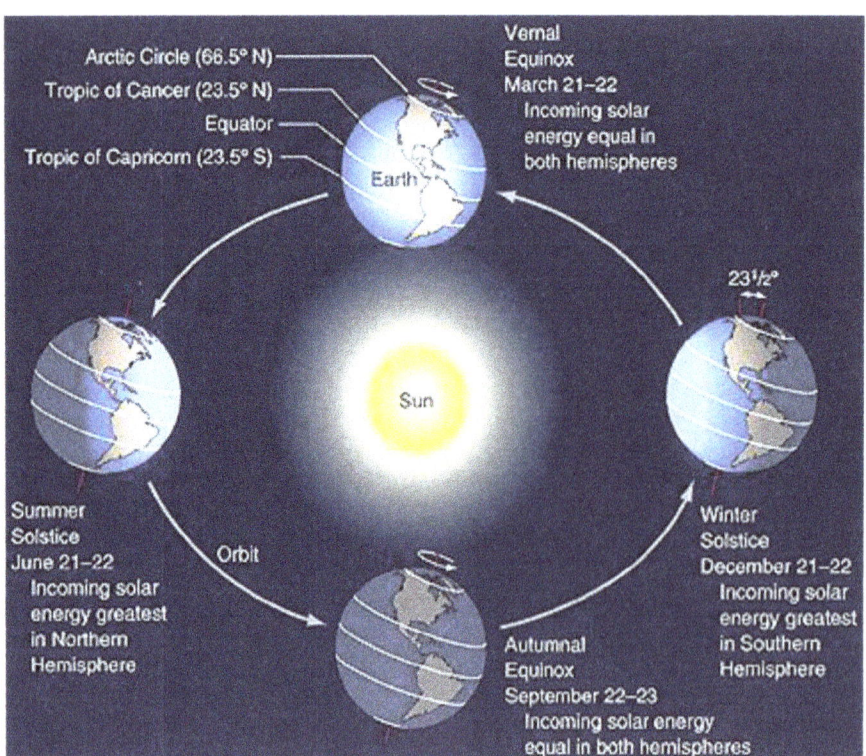

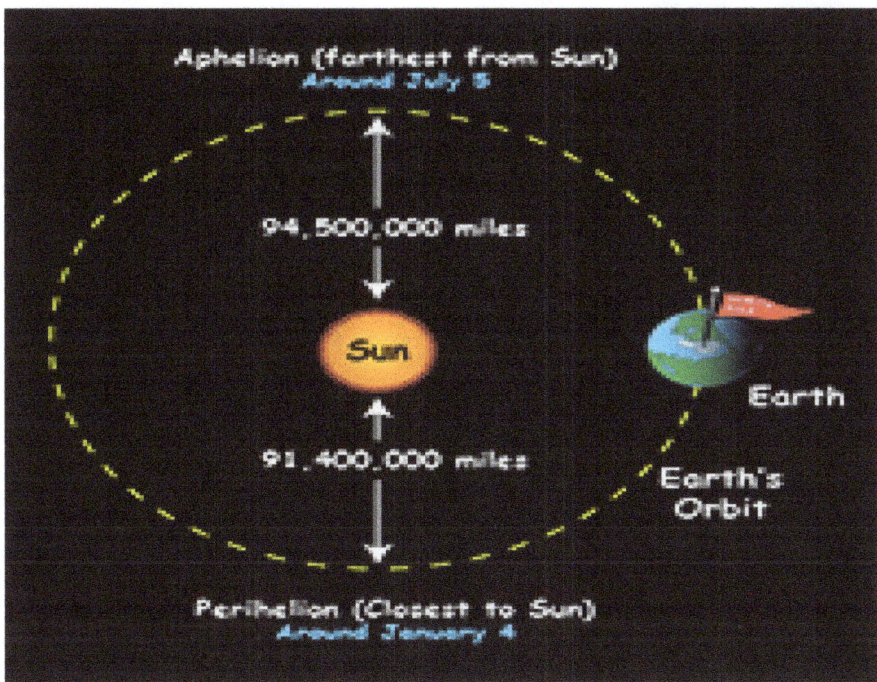

Retrieved from https://spaceplace.nasa.gov/seasons/en/

We are closer to the sun in the winter time….Now that was a surprise. If we were closer to the sun during the summer what would happen? If the angle of the earth were different, what would happen? You would think that these changes would totally change life on earth and possibly make life impossible.

"Sometimes it is the North Pole tilting toward the sun (around June) and sometimes it is the South Pole tilting toward the sun (around December)."

Retrieved from https://spaceplace.nasa.gov/seasons/en/

"Other planets in our solar system also tilt at various degrees. Uranus rotates almost sideways at 97 degrees and has extreme seasons. The axial tilt on Venus is 177.3 degrees. Hence, Venus has very little in the way of seasons."

Retrieved from http://earthsky.org/earth/can-you-explain-why-earth-has-four-seasons

If the earth were closer to, or farther from the sun, what would happen? "The water on Earth's surface covers about 70 percent of our planet and its atmosphere, and it is what makes Earth appear blue from outer space. ... If Earth were closer to the sun, however, the oceans would boil away. If it were farther away, the oceans would freeze."

Retrieved from https://science.howstuffworks.com/46001-earth-explained.htm

Consider these passages:

Job 38:32

> Do constellations of stars change over the different seasons?

Psalm 74:17

> Who made the seasons?

Jeremiah 8:7

> Do the birds know the seasons? What do birds do with the seasons?

If you live on the earth, you get four seasons. But not all places on the planet get the same amount of sun every year.

"There are only two times of the year when the Earth's axis is tilted neither toward nor away from the sun, resulting in a "nearly" equal amount of daylight and darkness at all latitudes. These events are referred to as Equinoxes. The word equinox is derived from two Latin words - aequus (equal) and nox (night). At the equator, the sun is directly overhead at noon on these two equinoxes. The "nearly" equal hours of day and night is due to refraction of sunlight or a bending of the light's rays that causes the sun to appear above the horizon when the actual position of the sun is below the horizon. Additionally, the days become a little longer at the higher latitudes (those at a distance from the equator) because it takes the sun longer to rise and set. Therefore, on the equinox and for several days before and after the equinox, the length of day will range from about 12 hours and six and one-half minutes at the equator, to 12 hours and 8 minutes at 30 degrees latitude, to 12 hours and 16 minutes at 60 degrees latitude."

Retrieved from https://www.weather.gov/cle/seasons

Two quotes from The Great Gatsby:

"And so with the sunshine and the great bursts of leaves growing on the trees, just as things grow in fast movies, I had that familiar conviction that life was beginning over again with the summer." — F. Scott Fitzgerald, The Great Gatsby

"Life starts all over again when it gets crisp in the fall." — F. Scott Fitzgerald, The Great Gatsby

Which season do you enjoy the most?

What is the benefit of people enjoying different seasons?

Does every season have a psychological advantage?

Does every season have an emotional advantage?

God is amazing with the seasons! It is spring in Muncie, as I am writing this, and weather reports are saying we could get 5-8 inches of snow tomorrow night. It is spring, and God is making it snow. We could get more snow in the spring this year than we did in the previous winter. Now that is amazing!

What creates a year on this planet? One orbit around the sun…This is a novel idea… Nicolai Copernicus (1473-1543) radically changed the understanding of astronomy when he proposed that the sun, not Earth, was the center of the solar system. This led to our modern understanding of the relationship between the sun and Earth.

The earth takes 365.25 days to orbit around the sun – this is a sidereal year. It will travel 92.96 million miles during this time period. Other planets in our solar system have different days in their years. Venus's year is 225 earth days. Mars' year is 687 earth days

What creates a day on this planet? One rotation on its axis…The days on this planet are amazing…Consider -- God's accuracy and consistency of days may be observed in the hatching of eggs.

-the eggs of the potato bug hatch in 7 days;
-those of the canary in 14 days;
-those of the barnyard hen in 21 days;
-The eggs of ducks and geese hatch in 28 days;
-those of the mallard in 35 days;
-The eggs of the parrot and the ostrich hatch in 42 days.

(Notice, they are all divisible by seven, the number of days in a week!)

Retrieved from https://www.allworship.com/gods-accuracy/

"One reason has to do with our climate. Our seasons are the result of our planet's tilt—when your part of the world tilts toward the sun, you get spring and summer; when it tilts away, you get fall and winter. God didn't have to do things this way—he could have created our planet with no tilt and thus no seasons. But then regions further from the equator would receive much less sunlight and thus be much less inhabitable. God loves diversity, and wanted us to experience our world from the far north to the far south."

Retrieved from http://www.christianheadlines.com/columnists/denison-forum/why-did-god-make-the-seasons.html

In closing -- look at what Solomon wrote about the seasons…

Song of Songs 2:10-13

10 My lover spoke and said to me, "Arise, my darling, my beautiful one, and come with me.

11 See! The winter is past; the rains are over and gone.

12 Flowers appear on the earth; the season of singing has come, the cooing of doves is heard in our land.

13 The fig tree forms its early fruit; the blossoming vines spread their fragrance. Arise, come, my darling; my beautiful one, come with me."

What season is Solomon writing about?

What did Solomon like about spring?

Was it the fragrances?

Was it the sounds?

Was it the leaves and fruit on the trees?

Can you relate to what Solomon wrote?

And the man wanted to share this with his beloved! God was using the seasons to bring them closer together!

In closing, what part of this study was:

Science based

Logic based

Evidence Enlightenment

Divine Design

Session 8

Crops and their seasons

Acts 14:17 "Yet he has not left himself without testimony: He has shown kindness by giving you rain from heaven and **crops in their seasons**; he provides you with plenty of food and fills your hearts with joy."

God, I am ok with three of the seasons, but do we really need the Winter? Let me confess that I think the person who invented wind chill should be shot. But according to Don Attwood, an ecological anthropologist at McGill University in Montreal,

"Winter protects much of the world's population from tropical insects (which carry deadly diseases) and a long, nasty list of tropical diseases of humans, crops and livestock. HIV is one virus that has escaped its tropical forest home. Many others, like the Ebola virus, are waiting for their chance," Attwood said. "Human mortality and morbidity rates (due directly to disease and indirectly to hunger) would go through the roof."

Retrieved from https://www.livescience.com/18972-earth-seasons-tilt.html

HIV and ebola are affected by the winter. Winter is like a vaccination against these two illnesses. Ok God thanks for the winter, and I guess the colder it gets the better it is. Farmers will say that we need cold, deep cold for a while to kill off insects etc.

I love the pictures of the seasons…

Psalm 1:3

What are the benefits of fruits having different growing seasons?

Let me bring this to home, my home….

CROP AREA #2 NORTHEAST INDIANA

Counties: Elkhart, Lagrange, Steuben, Kosciusko, Noble, Dekalb, Miami, Wabash, Huntington, Allen, Wells, Adams, Grant, Blackford, Jay, Madison, Delaware, Randolph, Henry, and Wayne

Vegetable Crops:

Asparagus May 1 – June 30

Cabbage April 15 – Oct. 1

Cucumbers / Pickles May 1 - July 15 Plant/Hoe
July 15 – Oct. 15 Harvest

Green Beans May 1 – July 15 Plant/Hoe
July 15 – Oct. 15 Harvest

Jalapeno Peppers April 30 – Oct. 1

Peppers April 30 – Oct. 1

Potatoes April 30 – Nov. 15

Pumpkins July 1 – Nov. 20

Onions June 15 – Nov. 1

Mint June 1 – July 10

Squash July 1 – Nov. 20

Sweet Corn July 10 – Nov. 1

Tomatoes May 1 – Aug. 15 Plant/Hoe
Aug – Oct. 15 Harvest

Tomato Processing Aug. 1 – Oct. 15

Fruit Crops:

Apples July 15 – Nov. 20 Harvest
Dec. 1 – Dec. 22 Prune
March 1 – March 30 Prune

Blueberries April 5 – Sept. 4

Cherries July 1 – Sept. 15

Pears Aug. 15 – Sept. 1
Dec. 5 – Dec. 22 Prune
March 3 – March 30 Prune

Peaches July 1 – Aug. 15
Dec. 5 – Dec. 22 Prune
March 3 – March 30 Prune

Plums Aug. 1 – Sept. 1
Dec. 5 – Dec. 22 Prune
March 3 – March 30 Prune

Strawberries May 20 – June 10

Other Crops:

Nursery March 15 – Nov. 30

Seed Corn July 1 – Aug. 1

Sod March 1 – Nov. 25

Retrieved from https://www.in.gov/dwd/2619.htm

Why do these crops have different growing seasons and times?

How does evolution account for this?

Is the song "America The Beautiful" correct?

"O beautiful for spacious skies
For amber waves of grain
For purple mountain majesties
Above the fruited plain!

America! America!
God shed his grace on thee
And crown thy good with brotherhood
From sea to shining sea!"

(Words by Katharine Lee Bates with melody by Samuel Ward)

What are "amber waves of grain"? Are the mountains majestic? What are "fruited plains"?

Top crops, in the world, counted down from #10 to #1

- Plantains
- Yams
- Sorghum
- Sweet Potatoes
- Soybeans
- Cassava
- Potatoes
- Rice
- Wheat
- Corn

Retrieved from http://www.businessinsider.com/10-crops-that-feed-the-world-2011-9#9-yams-2

Back to the Bible…

Ecclesiastes 3:1-11

- Do the seasons have different activities people take part in?
- What is the benefit of this?
- What would happen if you did the same outdoor activity year-round?
- Would you grow to hate it?

Genesis 8:22

    What is the guarantee of the seasons on this planet?

Matthew 24:32-33

    What lessons can we learn from the trees?

Psalms 104:19

    What marks off the seasons?

Genesis 1:14-19

    What marks off the seasons?

Consider this poem by Reginald Heber, "Spring," in The Christian Observer, January 1816

When Spring unlocks the flowers
To paint the laughing soil;
When summer's balmy breezes
Refresh the mower's toil;
When winter holds in frosty chains
The fallow and the flood;
In God the earth rejoices still,
And owns her Maker good.

And these quotes and poems:

"There is no season such delight can bring, As summer, autumn, winter, and the spring." William Browne

    Is William correct?

"We humans were clearly highly seasonal beasts until the coming of electric light but traces remain." Brian Follett

    Is Brian correct?

And the seasons affect our moods…

Forecast for spring: giddy and warm.
Forecast for summer: happy and hot.
Forecast for autumn: serene and chilly.
Forecast for winter: blessed and freezing.

By Terri Guillemets

So, do people have different seasons they like?

Which one is your favorite?

Is Terri correct about her adjectives for the seasons?

Spring is being blessed and happy,
with blooming flowers.
Summer is being blessed and hot,
with abundant sunshine.
Autumn is being blessed and reflective,
with colored leaves.
Winter is being blessed and chilly,
with sparkling snow.

By Terri Guillemets

Are all the seasons blessed?

Is the blessing an attitude?

What is seasonal affective disorder?

"The cold dull glow of winter warms to the colorful brilliance of springtime." Terri Guillemets

Do we appreciate spring more after having a harsh winter?

Do the sounds of the birds in spring brighten our mood?

Do people love listening to them?

And what about when you see the first robin of spring?

In closing, what part of this study was:

Science based

Logic based

Evidence Enlightenment

Divine Design

Session 9

Food glorious food

There is plenty of food on this planet. "There are over 20,000 species of edible plants in the world yet fewer than 20 species now provide 90% of our food. However, there are hundreds of less well known edible plants from all around the world which are both delicious and nutritious."

Retrieved from https://www.pfaf.org/user/edibleuses.aspx

This number is a testimony of God. Food demonstrates our dependence upon God. That thought should make us humble and turn us away from pride. Moses noted these truths when he reminded the Israelites of God's leading in their lives:

"He humbled you, causing you to hunger and then feeding you with manna, which neither you nor your ancestors had known, to teach you that man does not live on bread alone but on every word that comes from the mouth of the LORD" (Deuteronomy 8:3).

Food has 3 main functions in the body:

- Growth and Development
- Provision of Energy
- Repair and maintenance of the body's cells

Retrieved from http://9foodies.weebly.com/functions-of-food.html

Some strange facts about food:

Boys have fewer taste buds on the surface of their tongues than girls do.

Watermelon is the state vegetable of Oklahoma

Vegetables that are actually fruits:

- Tomatoes
- Cucumbers
- Courgetti
- Avocado
- Peppers

    Pumpkins

    Butternut squash

    Olives

    Aubergine

    Peapods

Retrieved from https://www.favrify.com/vegetables-that-are-fruits/

Is being hungry for food a testimony of God?

Why is eating a variety of fruits and vegetables important to the body? They have a wide variety of vitamins and minerals which are important to the body and the immune system.

Is it true that the brighter the colors of fruits and vegetables the better it is for your diet?

What would happen if we could not experience hunger?

What do most foods contain? Calories! Consider….

"Calories aren't bad for you. Your body needs calories for energy. But eating too many calories — and not burning enough of them off through activity — can lead to weight gain. Most foods and drinks contain calories."

Retrieved from kidshealth.org/en/kids/calorie.html

The body needs a variety of the following 5 nutrients - protein, carbohydrate, fat, vitamins and minerals - from the food we eat to stay healthy and productive.

Protein - is needed to build, maintain and repair muscle, blood, skin and bones and other tissues and organs in the body.

Foods rich in protein include meat, eggs, dairy and fish.

Carbohydrate - provides the body with its main source of energy. Carbohydrates can be classified into two kinds; starches and sugars.

Food rich in starches include rice, maize, wheat and potatoes and food rich in sugars include fruit, honey, sweets and chocolate bars.

Fat - This is the body's secondary source of energy. Fat actually provides more energy/calories per gram than any other nutrient, but is more difficult to burn.

Food rich in fats are oils, butter, lard, milk, cheese and some meat.

Vitamins and Minerals – Vitamins and minerals are needed in very small amounts and are sometimes called micronutrients, but are essential for good health. They control many functions and processes in the body, and in the case of minerals also help build body tissue such as bones (calcium) and blood (iron).

Fiber and Water are also essential for a good healthy diet.

Retrieved from https://www.concern.net/sites/default/files/media/page/Hunger_Factsheets.pdf

So, what happens if there is a mineral or vitamin deficiency in the body?

What happens if people eat too much sugar? Is sugar addictive?

Are there food allergies? Two types of allergies are acute and delayed. Acute is like an instant reaction. Delayed can be a reaction days later. Should people eat gluten? Does what we eat affect our brain? Is inflammation of the body a warning sign? What is celiac disease? It is a wheat sensitivity.

"Celiac disease is a serious autoimmune disorder that can occur in genetically predisposed people where the ingestion of gluten leads to damage in the small intestine. It is estimated to affect 1 in 100 people worldwide. Two and one-half million Americans are undiagnosed and are at risk for long-term health complications."

Retrieved from https://celiac.org/celiac-disease/understanding-celiac-disease-2/what-is-celiac-disease/#xgXgvmUzRHIZgQbV.99

How dangerous are processed foods for the body?

Is a low-fat diet dangerous for the brain?

Back to things that are amazing about food:

What about the taste of food? What would happen if all food tasted the same?

What about the texture of food? What would happen if all food had the same texture?

Would you eat your favorite picnic meal, hot dog with relish on the bun with baked beans and potato salad, after it all was thrown into a blender and pureed? Why or why not? Does the idea of drinking your meal gross you out? Why or why not?

Are taste and texture testimonies of God? A lot of people like food because of the taste or texture. Consider, "But how a food feels affects our enjoyment of the thing. There is, of course, the actual texture of the food, which scientists call rheology. Rheology focuses on consistency and flow. ... Texture is an important indicator of a food's fat content."

Retrieved from https://www.popsci.com/texture-food-science

And what about the smell of food?

"Problems with these senses have a big impact on our lives. Smell and taste contribute to our enjoyment of life by stimulating a desire to eat which not only nourishes our bodies, but also enhances our social activities. When smell and taste become impaired, we eat poorly, socialize less, and feel worse. Smell and taste warn us of dangers, such as fire, poisonous fumes, and spoiled food. Loss of the sense of smell may indicate sinus disease, growths in the nasal passages, or, at times, brain tumors."

Retrieved from http://www.entnet.org/content/smell-taste

Food and Fellowship are two of my favorite things. Look at the early church:

Acts 2:42-47; 20:7 God created food for fellowship.

What foods do you not like because of the texture or taste? Mine is coconut. It is slimy. My wife's best friend Carla hates seafood. My wife Janelle and I love seafood!

And our bodies can digest food. That's a miracle of itself. And our body can eliminate the waste.

> All parts of the body (muscles, brain, heart, and liver) need energy to work. This energy comes from the food we eat.
>
> Our bodies digest the food we eat by mixing it with fluids (acids and enzymes) in the stomach. When the stomach digests food, the carbohydrate (sugars and starches) in the food breaks down into another type of sugar, called glucose.
>
> The stomach and small intestines absorb the glucose and then release it into the bloodstream. Once in the bloodstream, glucose can be used immediately for energy or stored in our bodies, to be used later.
>
> However, our bodies need insulin in order to use or store glucose for energy. Without insulin, glucose stays in the bloodstream, keeping blood sugar levels high.

Retrieved from https://wa.kaiserpermanente.org/healthAndWellness?item=%2Fcommon%2FhealthAndWellness%2Fconditions%2Fdiabetes%2FfoodProcess.html

Our body has organs that help digest food:

>Liver
>Pancreas
>Gallbladder

Our body also has:

> The mouth
> Esophagus
> Stomach
> Small intestine
> Large intestine

Our body is also designed to eliminate waste. Consider...

"If urine could not be released, pressure would back up the ureters into the kidneys, ultimately destroying them. If the individual did not get hemodialysis, he/she would die of renal failure, especially from the toxicity of nitrogenous wastes to the brain."

Retrieved from https://www.quora.com/What-would-happen-if-the-human-body-didnt-release-their-waste-urine-and-poop

What would happen if the colon did not eliminate waste? You would think the colon would become so large it would have to be removed by surgery. The pain would be amazing. Just think about the amount of gas you would have. A small passing of gas through an impacted colon could probably clear a room. If the colon did not eliminate waste, it would eventually burst and put putrefied waste all throughout the abdominal cavity. This would produce infection like gangrene. This could not be healthy for the body...

"Gangrene refers to the death of body tissue due to either a lack of blood flow or a serious bacterial infection. Gangrene commonly affects the extremities, including your toes, fingers and limbs, but it can also occur in your muscles and internal organs."

Retrieved from https://www.mayoclinic.org/diseases-conditions/gangrene/symptoms-causes/syc-20352567

I guess we are lucky we can eliminate waste.

Consider this table about how the body eliminates waste:

Organ(s)	Function	Component of Other Organ System
Lungs	Remove carbon dioxide.	Respiratory system
Skin	Sweat glands remove water, salts, and other wastes.	Integumentary system
Large intestine	Removes solid waste and some water in the form of feces.	Digestive system

Organ(s)	Function	Component of Other Organ System
Kidneys	Remove urea, salts, and excess water from the blood.	Urinary system

Retrieved from https://www.ck12.org/biology/excretory-system/lesson/Excretion-MS-LS/

The Bible mentions a lot of foods:

FRUITS AND NUTS

- Apples (Song of Solomon 2:5)
- Almonds (Genesis 43:11; Numbers 17:8)
- Dates (2 Samuel 6:19; 1 Chronicles 16:3)
- Figs (Nehemiah 13:15; Jeremiah 24:1-3)
- Grapes (Leviticus 19:10; Deuteronomy 23:24)
- Melons (Numbers 11:5; Isaiah 1:8)
- Olives (Isaiah 17:6; Micah 6:15)
- Pistachio Nuts (Genesis 43:11)
- Pomegranates (Numbers 20:5; Deuteronomy 8:8)
- Raisins (Numbers 6:3; 2 Samuel 6:19)
- Sycamore Fruit (Psalm 78:47; Amos 7:14)

VEGETABLES AND LEGUMES

- Beans (2 Samuel 17:28; Ezekiel 4:9)
- Cucumbers (Numbers 11:5)
- Gourds (2 Kings 4:39)
- Leeks (Numbers 11:5)
- Lentils (Genesis 25:34; 2 Samuel 17:28; Ezekiel 4:9)
- Onions (Numbers 11:5)

GRAINS

- Barley (Deuteronomy 8:8; Ezekiel 4:9)
- Bread (Genesis 25:34; 2 Samuel 6:19; 16:1; Mark 8:14)
- Corn (Matthew 12:1; KJV - refers to "grain" such as wheat or barley)

- Flour (2 Samuel 17:28; 1 Kings 17:12)
- Millet (Ezekiel 4:9)
- Spelt (Ezekiel 4:9)
- Unleavened Bread (Genesis 19:3; Exodus 12:20)
- Wheat (Ezra 6:9; Deuteronomy 8:8)

FISH

- Matthew 15:36
- John 21:11-13

FOWL

- Partridge (1 Samuel 26:20; Jeremiah 17:11)
- Pigeon (Genesis 15:9; Leviticus 12:8)
- Quail (Psalm 105:40)
- Dove (Leviticus 12:8)

ANIMAL MEATS

- Calf (Proverbs 15:17; Luke 15:23)
- Goat (Genesis 27:9)
- Lamb (2 Samuel 12:4)
- Oxen (1 Kings 19:21)
- Sheep (Deuteronomy 14:4)
- Venison (Genesis 27:7 KJV)

DAIRY

- Butter (Proverbs 30:33)
- Cheese (2 Samuel 17:29; Job 10:10)
- Curds (Isaiah 7:15)
- Milk (Exodus 33:3; Job 10:10; Judges 5:25)

MISCELLANEOUS

- Eggs (Job 6:6; Luke 11:12)
- Grape Juice (Numbers 6:3)
- Honey (Exodus 33:3; Deuteronomy 8:8; Judges 14:8-9)
- Locust (Mark 1:6)
- Olive Oil (Ezra 6:9; Deuteronomy 8:8)
- Vinegar (Ruth 2:14; John 19:29)
- Wine (Ezra 6:9; John 2:1-10)

What does Genesis 26:12 teach about food and God?

What are the five major food groups?

1. **Grains** (includes bread and cereals)
2. **Vegetables**
3. **Fruits**
4. **Milk and Dairy** (including cheese)
5. **Meat and Beans** (includes fish, poultry, and eggs)

Our planet grows all of them…..in abundance….Genesis 27:28; 41:48; Job 36:31. God's blessings to us come from the bountiful abundance of everything found on this planet that God gave us for life.

What does Genesis 4:2-3; 9:20 teach about food?

What about the Daniel diet -- Daniel 1:12-16, "Please test your servants for ten days: Give us nothing but vegetables to eat and water to drink. Then compare our appearance with that of the young men who eat the royal food and treat your servants in accordance with what you see." So he agreed to this and tested them for ten days. At the end of the ten days they looked healthier and better nourished than any of the young men who ate the royal food. So the guard took away their choice food and the wine they were to drink and gave them vegetables instead."

Why is food important?

What does food contain? Vitamins. Consider where they come from and what they do!

"11 Essential Vitamins and Minerals Your Body Needs"

We all know vitamins and minerals are essential nutrients the body needs - but what does each vitamin do? And which foods are vitamin powerhouses? Here's the low-down on which letter does what, from A (that is, Vitamin A) to Z (or - zinc).

1. VITAMIN A

GOOD FOR: Healthy eyes and general growth and development, including healthy teeth and skin.

NATURAL SOURCE: Carrots and other orange foods including sweet potato and cantaloupe melons – all of which get their hue from the carotene pigment.

2. B VITAMINS

GOOD FOR: Energy production, immune function and iron absorption.

NATURAL SOURCE: This crucial group of nutrients can be found in whole unprocessed foods, specifically whole grains, potatoes, bananas, lentils, chili peppers, beans, yeast and molasses.

3. VITAMIN C

GOOD FOR: Strengthening blood vessels and giving skin its elasticity, anti-oxidant function and iron absorption.

NATURAL SOURCE: Everyone knows this one – oranges! But they're not the only source – other fruits and veggies packed with Vitamin C include guava, red and green peppers, kiwi, grapefruits, strawberries, Brussels sprouts and cantaloupe.

4. VITAMIN D

GOOD FOR: Strong healthy bones.

NATURAL SOURCE: Apart from spending a few minutes out in the sun, which stimulates Vitamin D production, you can get this nutritional must from eggs, fish and mushrooms.

5. VITAMIN E

GOOD FOR: Blood circulation, and protection from free radicals.

NATURAL SOURCE: Our favorite Vitamin E-rich food is the mighty almond. You can also fill up on other nuts, sunflower seeds and tomatoes to reap the benefits.

6. VITAMIN K

GOOD FOR: Blood coagulation – that is, the process by which your blood clots.

NATURAL SOURCE: Leafy greens are the best natural sources of Vitamin K – so make sure you're eating lots of kale, spinach, Brussels sprouts and broccoli.

7. FOLIC ACID

GOOD FOR: Cell renewal and preventing birth defects in pregnancy.

NATURAL SOURCE: There are plenty of scrumptious natural sources of folic acid, including dark leafy greens, asparagus, broccoli, citrus fruits, beans, peas, lentils, seeds, nuts, cauliflower, beets and corn.

8. CALCIUM

GOOD FOR: Healthy teeth and bones.

NATURAL SOURCE: This mineral is another one that most of us already know - the best sources are dairy products like yogurt, cheese and milk, along with tofu and black molasses.

9. IRON

GOOD FOR: Building muscles naturally and maintaining healthy blood.

NATURAL SOURCE: You might be surprised to know that clams take the top spot for iron content, followed by oysters and organ meats like liver. For the vegetarians among us, soybeans, cereal, pumpkin seeds, beans, lentils and spinach are great sources of iron.

10. ZINC

GOOD FOR: Immunity, growth and fertility.

NATURAL SOURCE: Seafoods like oysters are also zinc-rich, along with spinach, cashews, beans and – wait for it – dark chocolate.

11. CHROMIUM

GOOD FOR: Glucose function – making sure every cell in your body gets energy as and when needed.

NATURAL SOURCE: As long as your diet contains servings of whole grains, fresh vegetables and herbs, you should be getting enough chromium.

Retrieved from https://www.goodnet.org/articles/11-essential-vitamins-minerals-your-body-needs

Plants and their leaves are not just for food but also for medicine. Ezekiel 47:12 makes an amazing statement, "And by the river upon the bank thereof, on this side and on that side, shall grow all trees for meat, whose leaf shall not fade, neither shall the fruit thereof be consumed: it shall bring forth new fruit according to his months, because their waters they issued out of the sanctuary: and the fruit thereof shall be for meat, and the leaf thereof for medicine." KJV

Leaf-based medicines… consider what Hippocrates said, "Let thy food be thy medicine and thy medicine be thy food." From Revelation 22:2, what were the leaves used for?

Consider looking this up…."Why Plants Are (Usually) Better Than Drugs" By Dr. Andrew Weil

Retrieved from https://www.huffingtonpost.com/andrew-weil-md/why-plants-are-usually-be_b_785139.html

And what about essential oils and aromatherapy? Dr. David Steward Ph.D. in "Healing Oils of the Bible" has a list of specific Biblical references to Essential Oils and/or Aromatic plants (He lists 261 citations and 33 Species.)

Consider these statements about food-mood connection. "You probably know that the food you eat affects your body. Many studies have shown the connection between your food choices and your overall health. Eating a nutritious diet helps you keep a healthy body weight and a healthy heart. It also helps reduce your risk of developing some chronic diseases. New research finds that your food choices may also affect your mood and mental health. This is sometimes called the "food-mood connection."

Retrieved from https://familydoctor.org/nutrition-mental-health/

"Finally, while there are yet to be published RCTs testing dietary improvement as a treatment strategy for depression, the first of these is underway and results will be published within six months."

Retrieved from http://www.ncbi.nlm.nih.gov/pmc/articles/PMC3636120/

There are also now two interventions suggesting that dietary improvement can prevent depression:

Retrieved from http://www.ncbi.nlm.nih.gov/pmc/articles/PMC3848350/
Retrieved from http://www.ncbi.nlm.nih.gov/pmc/articles/PMC4050338/

"12 Foods to Boost Your Mood & Energy!"

Salmon. Salmon is a great source of the energy-boosting goodness that is essential omega-3 fatty acids, which are important for energy production, brain activity and circulation. ...

Banana. Bananas are one of the world's best foods for supplying your body with energy. ...

Coconut. ...

Lentils. ...

Eggs. ...

Kale. ...

Ginger Tea. ...

Nuts.

Retrieved from www.foodmatters.com/article/12-foods-to-boost-your-mood-energy

"10 Healthy Foods That Give You Energy"

Oatmeal. Start your morning off with whole grains. ...

Yogurt. If you're looking for a quick boost before a workout, yogurt is an easy grab-and-go snack. ...

Shrimp. Shrimp are low in calories and contain vitamin B12, which helps with energy metabolism. ...

Strawberries. ...

Hummus. ...

Spinach. ...

Almonds. ...

Bananas.

Retrieved from www.mensfitness.com/nutrition/what-to-eat/10-healthy-foods-give-you-energy

"8 Health Benefits of Raw Honey"

Healthy Weight Management.

Counters Pollen Allergies.

Natural Energy Source.

Antioxidant Powerhouse.

Sleep Promoter.

Wound and Ulcer Healer.

Diabetes Aid.

Natural Cough Syrup.

Retrieved from https://draxe.com/the-many-health-benefits-of-raw-honey/

"What Are Cherries Good For? -- Health Benefits of Cherries" by Dr. Mercola

"Antioxidant Protection. Cherries contain powerful antioxidants like anthocyanins and cyanidin."

Cancer-Preventive Compounds. ...

Reduce Inflammation and Your Risk of Gout. ...

Support Healthy Sleep (Melatonin) ...

Arthritis Pain Relief. ...

Reduce Belly Fat. ...

Reduce Post-Exercise Muscle Pain. ...

Lower Risk of Stroke.

Retrieved from https://articles.mercola.com/sites/articles/archive/2014/08/.../health-benefits-cherries.aspx

What happened to Jonathan when he ate honey? 1 Samuel 14:29

How was the promised land described? Numbers 14:8; Jeremiah 11:5

What does Proverbs teach about honey? Proverbs 24:13; 25:16

Consider this diagram about what food does for the body…

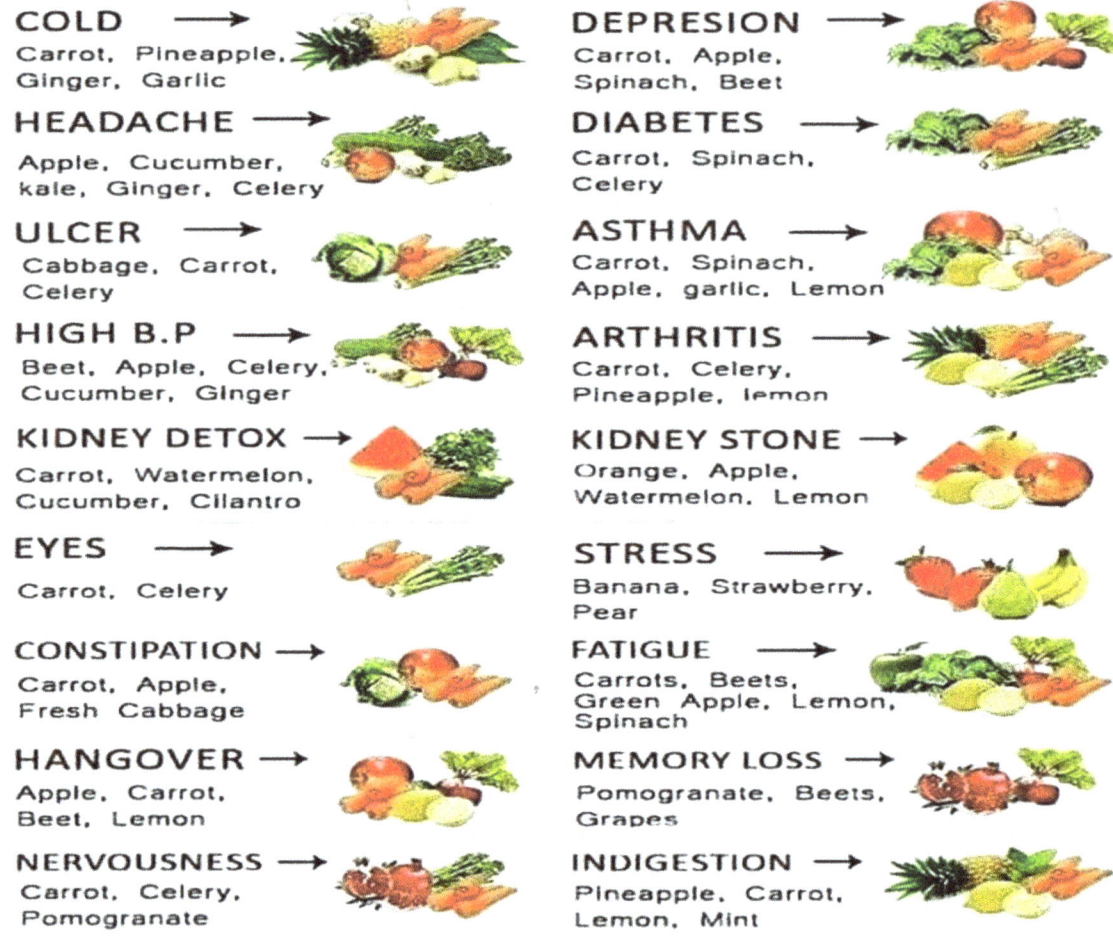

"Superfoods' Everyone Needs"

Blueberries -- Antioxidant Superfood

Omega 3-Rich Fish -- Superfoods for the Heart, Joints, and Memory

Soy -- Superfood to Lower Cholesterol

Fiber -- Superfood Aids Weight Loss and Checks Cholesterol

Tea -- Superfood for Lowering Cholesterol and Inhibiting Cancer

Calcium

And Finally, the Yummiest Superfood Yet ... Dark Chocolate

Retrieved from http://www.webmd.com/diet/features/superfoods-everyone-needs? February 2007.

Dr. Lorenzo Cohen explains the power of healthy choices.

"The American Cancer Society and the American Institute for Cancer Research both estimate that more than 30% of cancer can be prevented through healthy diet, physical activity, and maintaining a healthy weight. Smoking also accounts for over 30% of cancers. This means that through appropriate lifestyle choices, more than 50% of cancers and cancer-related deaths could be avoided."

Retrieved from http://www.dbadocket.org/work-life-balance/food-as-medicine-can-you-eat-your-way-to-better-health/

In the article "Culinary Medicine: Healing Yourself With Food," Dr. John La Puma reiterates that food is the best way to "prevent, treat and even reverse illnesses" like diabetes, arthritis, metabolic syndrome, heart disease and depression. To reap the nutritious benefits available, he recommends eating superfoods full of antioxidants, anti-inflammatory properties, fiber and omega-3s.

Although there are many foods that could be considered "super," I chose to examine seven of the more common ones for you to easily incorporate into your everyday diet.

Garlic: During World War II, garlic was given to soldiers to prevent gangrene, and it was used as an antiseptic on wounds to prevent infection. Today, studies have shown that the antioxidants in garlic fight off harmful "free radicals" that build up in your body over time. It helps to prevent several ailments and diseases such as the common cold, heart disease and cancer. Garlic can also act as a blood thinner, preventing heart attacks and strokes. So next time your date gives you a hard time for garlic breath, dazzle them with your knowledge and good health!

Eat it now: Enjoy a White Garlic and Herb Bean Dip with veggies.

Honey: Known for its antibacterial and anti-inflammatory properties, honey is considered one of nature's "best all-around remedies" by holistic practitioners. It's made up of glucose and fructose, as well as minerals like iron, calcium, phosphate, sodium chlorine, potassium and magnesium. According to an article in Medical News Today, "The ancient Greeks believed that consuming honey could help you live longer." Apart from that perk, honey is also said to help in healing wounds, treating infections and allergies and preventing acid reflux. Pretty sweet!

Eat it now: Mix a little honey into your tea or Greek yogurt for a tasty snack. Or, make homemade Honey Almond Granola.

Apples: "An apple a day keeps the doctor away." There's a reason this catchy adage has stuck around for so long: It's true! One medium apple counts as one cup of fruit, and packs a nutritious punch of soluble fiber and vitamin C. In a study reported by EatingWell, apples were found to be associated with a lower risk of coronary heart disease and cardiovascular disease. And its heart-healthy benefits don't stop there—apples have also been shown to lower cholesterol levels.

Eat it now: Dip apple slices in almond or peanut butter to add protein.

Berries: Registered Dietitian Lauri Boone says that berries "top the charts with their high levels of antioxidants and phytochemicals to keep your brain young, skin glowing, and reduce your risk of heart disease, diabetes and cancer." These health benefits are found in the more common berries such as blackberries, raspberries, strawberries, blueberries and cranberries, along with others such as boysenberries, acai berries and goji berries.

Eat it now: Blend berries in a healthy smoothie, top frozen yogurt with them for a sweet dessert, or make Blueberry Baked Oatmeal to start your morning off right.

Eggs: Let's clear up this yolky hearsay right from the start: egg yolks are not the enemy. Whole eggs—including the yolk—are one of the best sources of choline, a nutrient proved to reduce a woman's chances of breast cancer. And, egg yolks are high in lutein and zeaxanthin, two antioxidants that protect against vision loss. Overall, one egg contains six grams of high-quality protein and all nine essential amino acids. So get cracking!

Eat it now: Mix a few eggs together with sausage and veggies for a tasty breakfast scramble, or go all out with a Bacon, Egg and Asparagus Pizza.

Salmon: It's hard to top the omega 3 levels found in salmon! This essential fatty acid is not produced by the body, and so eating salmon is an excellent way to get this necessary dose of nutrients. Omega 3 protects heart and brain health, improves blood vessel function and blood lipid (cholesterol), improves immune and inflammatory disorders and promotes healthy joints and skin.

Eat it now: Make Bourbon-glazed Salmon (and drink bourbon while cooking it—everything in moderation!).

Arugula: Leafy green with a bite, this plant-based vegetable contains cancer-fighting enzymes. The American Dietary Guidelines recommends that half of your plate consist of fruits and vegetables, and arugula is a great choice. Just one cup a day can make a big difference!

Eat it now: Switch up dinner with arugula pesto, or combine superfoods for a super lunch: Arugula, Avocado and Radish Salad with Poached Egg.

Retrieved from http://www.dbadocket.org/work-life-balance/food-as-medicine-can-you-eat-your-way-to-better-health/

Earlier this site mentioned apples…They are amazing… Consider there are:

"2,500 varieties of apples are grown in the United States. 7,500 varieties of apples are grown throughout the world. 100 varieties of apples are grown commercially in the United States."

Retrieved from https://extension.illinois.edu/apples/facts.cfm

Whether meat, seafood, vegetables, fruits, etc. All food is more than a source of energy. It is a blessing from the Lord. When Scripture talks about food it's not always talking about the physical. Sometimes it is talking about the spiritual and the spiritual food is something that most people neglect. That is why many are not healthy.

I love the writing of C. S. Lewis

"A man can eat his dinner without understanding exactly how food nourishes him." C.S. Lewis

"If we will not learn to eat the only food that the universe grows, then we must starve eternally." C.S. Lewis

God has given both believers and unbelievers food to eat. Consider what these passages teach.

Bible verses about food and eating

Psalm 146:7

    What three things does God do from this passage?

Genesis 9:3

    What are living creatures to be used for?

    How does this relate to:

        Genesis 1:11, 29-30

        Leviticus 3:17; 11:2, 10-11

        Romans 14:21

        1 Corinthians 8:13

Psalm 145:15

    Who is the three "you" in this passage?

Psalm 136:25

    What does God give to every creature?

In closing, what part of this study was:

Science based

Logic based

Evidence Enlightenment

Divine Design

Session 10

Let's be honest food is amazing

I love this article's title, "Jesus ate his way through the gospels – eaten with a tax-collector recently?"

"Ever noticed how many of Jesus' meals are in the gospels? Meals feature so prominently in the gospels that scholars have commented: 'Jesus ate his way through the Gospels.' Herbert Anderson and Edward Foley even claim: '… they killed him because of the way he ate; because he ate and drank with sinners.' Jesus revealed the Kingdom as he shared meals with others. And Jesus' 'fellowship meals' are formative for the mission of the local church today."

Retrieved from https://markrglanville.wordpress.com/2012/07/20/jesus-ate-his-way-through-the-gospels-eaten-with-a-tax-collector-recently/

Consider these food stories:

    Matthew 9:10-17

        What did Jesus' disciples not do?

    Mark 2:15-22

        Who did Jesus eat with?

        Who questioned Jesus doing this?

    Luke 5:29-39

        Who held a banquet for Jesus?

        What did this man do for a living?

    Luke 11:37-54

        Who invited Jesus to eat in this story?

Luke 14:1-24

> Who invited Jesus to eat in this story?
>
> What was the day of this meal?

Luke 24:30

> Who did Jesus eat with in this story?

Luke 24:41-43

> What question did Jesus ask the disciples?
>
> Did this prove he was alive?

Food is amazing…We need to find the wonder of it. Food is wonderful…full of wonder. What do these passages teach about wonders and miracles?

John 4:48

> What are the blessings of wonders and miraculous signs?

John 14:11

> What did Jesus say that the miracles have or show?

Job 5:9

> From this passage, what two things does God do?
>
> Why cannot the wonders be fathomed?
>
> Why cannot the miracles be counted?
>
> How does this relate to Psalm 40:5?

Job 37:14-15

> What did Elihu instruct Job to do?
>
> What did he want Job to consider in Job 37:15?

Psalm 89:5

> How does heaven praise God's wonder?

Psalm 105:5

> What three things should we remember?
>
> Which do we remember the most?

Psalm 119:27

> What does it mean to meditate on God's wonders?
>
> How often do we do this?

Preston Yancy's quote is amazing, "God hasn't stopped being a God of wonders. We stopped being a people who wanted to wonder in the first place."

> Has modern education stopped people from wondering?
>
> Has education and the way it teaches people to think, stopped people from wondering?

Consider what St. Augustine wrote, "Men go abroad to wonder at the heights of mountains, at the huge waves of the sea, at the long courses of the rivers, at the vast compass of the ocean, at the circular motions of the stars, and they pass by themselves without wondering."

Retrieved from https://www.classicalpursuits.com/programs/augustines-confessions/

And what happens if people don't get the food that they need? "Although not as critical as going without water, missing even just a few meals can cause a host of undesirable complications for the would-be survivor. Although we will not starve while going without food for several days or even a week, being underfed for even just one day can cause:

- Irritability
- Low moral
- Lethargy
- Physical Weakness
- Confusion and disorientation
- Poor judgment
- Weakened immune system
- Inability to maintain body temperature which can lead to hypothermia, heat exhaustion, or even heat stroke.

Retrieved from https://www.chippewahd.com/cms/lib/MI17000311/Centricity/Domain/22/Food_Shortages_and_Symptoms_of_Inadequate_Food_Consumption.pdf

So, does this make Matthew 6:11 more of an amazing teaching? What does this passage request? How does this relate to Proverbs 30:8?

What does Psalm 33:18-19 teach?

What does Psalm 34:10 express?

What does Isaiah 33:16 teach?

What does 1 Timothy 6:8 teach?

Who did God give food to?

    Exodus 16:12

        When God gave bread what should those who eat it realize?

Exodus 16:8

> What did Moses state that he wants the people to realize?

Why were the people grumbling?

Food is a gift from God to the Israelites, all the years that the Israelites were in the wilderness God fed them with manna. (Exodus 16:1-36; Numbers 11:7-9; Joshua 5:10-12)

What did Jesus call manna in John 6:31?

And the Bible has a great diet. It is referred to as the Daniel Diet. It is found in Daniel 1:11-16. I have done this diet for 10 days and I lost weight and inches. I am presently doing a modified version of it. I am feeling better. This diet affected their appearance and health. It is a high plant-based diet. This diet is first found in Genesis 1:29-30.

Plants on this planet need several things to grow

Air -- carbon dioxide
Water
Light
Nutrients
Soil
(And all of these just happen to be here on the earth!)

What is soil? It is "The unconsolidated mineral or organic material on the immediate surface of the Earth that serves as a natural medium for the growth of land plants."

Retrieved from http://www.mbmg.mtech.edu/kids/frequently-asked-questions.htm

So, what is a natural medium? How did this natural medium come to be? Let's think about soil

- Soil makes up the outermost layer of our planet.
- Topsoil is the most productive soil layer.
- Soil has varying amounts of organic matter (living and dead organisms), minerals, and nutrients.
- Natural processes can take more than 500 years to form one inch of topsoil.
- Soil scientists have identified over 70,000 kinds of soil in the United States.
- Soil is formed from rocks and decaying plants and animals.
- An average soil sample is 45 percent minerals, 25 percent water, 25 percent air, and five percent organic matter.

- Different-sized mineral particles, such as sand, silt, and clay, give soil its texture.
- Fungi and bacteria help break down organic matter in the soil.
- Plant roots and lichens break up rocks which become part of new soil.
- Roots loosen the soil, allowing oxygen to penetrate. This benefits animals living in the soil.
- Roots hold soil together and help prevent erosion.
- Five to 10 tons of animal life can live in an acre of soil.
- Earthworms digest organic matter, recycle nutrients, and make the surface soil richer.
- Mice take seeds and other plant materials into underground burrows, where this material eventually decays and becomes part of the soil.
- Mice, moles, and shrews dig burrows which help aerate the soil.

Retrieved from http://www.epa.gov/gmpo/edresources/soil.html

Is soil a testimony of God?

What is soil on this planet? "What are the different layers of soil?"

Soil Horizons (layers): Soil is made up of distinct horizontal layers; these layers are called horizons. They range from rich, organic upper layers (humus and topsoil) to underlying rocky layers (subsoil, regolith and bedrock).

www.enchantedlearning.com/geology/soil/

Let's look at another amazing testimony of God connected to food. It is the seed. Soil is nothing without the seed. It is amazing to comprehend that every plant and animal on this planet can reproduce. Plants reproduce by their seed.

Farmer Ted (a real man, who let me participate in his harvest, Ok, he let me ride in his combine), has taught me a lot about seeds. You can put it in the ground at the correct depth and the seed knows to grow the sprout up and the root down. Every seed "knows" this.

How does the seed know this?

Where did this preprogramed knowledge come from? "In botany, the 'radicle' is the first part of a seedling (a growing plant embryo) to emerge from the seed during the process of germination. The 'radicle' is the embryonic root of the plant, and grows downward in the soil (the shoot emerges from the plumule).

Retrieved from https://www7.dict.cc/wp_examples.php?lp_id=1&lang=en&s=radicle

This, just by itself, tells me there is a Divine design within the seed. FIY: seeds germinate at 55 degrees and the best soil temperatures for growth is between 55-85 degrees. (Thanks farmer Ted)

What does Genesis 1:11-12, 29 teach about the seed?

Is the seed living? Is it like an embryo?

Does the quality of the seed matter?

Seeds can be modified to make healthier plants. The science that does this is amazing. It is called genetically modified organisms, GMO's.

Also, consider what happens when you eat seeds. They are good for your health. Consider this article: "The 10 Healthiest Seeds on Earth"

> A seed is life. It is a living food. It is impossible to eat a raw seed and not derive nutrition. Many seeds are edible and the majority of human calories come from seeds, especially from legumes and nuts. Seeds also provide most cooking oils, many beverages and spices and some important food additives. In different seeds the seed embryo or the endosperm dominates and provides most of the nutrients. The storage proteins of the embryo and endosperm differ in their amino acid content and physical properties.
>
> How to Eat Seeds
>
> There is only one way to derive nutrition from seeds and that is to eat them raw. Once they are exposed to heat, they produce toxic substances and the vitamin, mineral and essential oil profiles are denatured. By roasting a seed, it's classification moves from a living food to a dead food. There is no seed on earth that can withstand roasting or heating without breaking down its nutritional components. Always remember, eat seeds naturally…eat them raw. This also means they can be soaked, ground or mashed (i.e. tahini), especially if a seed's shell or coat is too difficult to pierce with the teeth.
>
> - Choose raw and unsalted seeds
> - Avoid coated or roasted seeds
> - Avoid sugar coated seeds

Retrieved from https://realfarmacy.com/the-top-10-healthiest-seeds-on-earth/

More about seeds:

"The 10 Healthiest Seeds on Earth"

1) Chia seeds
2) Hemp seeds
3) Pomegranate seeds
4) Flax seeds
5) Pumpkin seeds
6) Apricot seeds
7) Sesame seeds
8) Sunflower seeds
9) Cumin seeds
10) Grape seeds

Retrieved from http://preventdisease.com/news/13/021913_The-Top-10-Healthiest-Seeds-on-Earth.shtml

Are seeds a testimony of God? Does a person get the same nutrition from eating the seeds as from eating the plant? Does a person get nutrition from eating the leaves of a plant? What are the parts of a seed? "The outside covering of seeds is called the seed coat. It protects the baby plant, or embryo, inside the seed. The seed also contains endosperm, or a food supply, that the embryo uses to grow until the plant can manufacture its own food."

Retrieved from http://sciencenetlinks.com/lessons/look-at-those-seeds-grow/

The seed contains its own food supply – is that amazing?

The plant can manufacture its own food?

How does the plant do this?

> Plants are called autotrophs because they can use energy from light to synthesize, or make, their own food source. Many people believe they are "feeding" a plant when they put it in soil, water it, or place it outside in the Sun, but none of these things are considered food. Rather, plants use sunlight, water, and the gases in the air to make glucose, which is a form of sugar that plants need to survive. This process is called photosynthesis and is performed by all plants, algae, and even some microorganisms. To perform photosynthesis, plants need three things: carbon dioxide, water, and sunlight.

Retrieved from https://ssec.si.edu/stemvisions-blog/what-photosynthesis

So, does photosynthesis occur by accident or by design?

In closing, what part of this study was:

Science based

Logic based

Evidence Enlightenment

Divine Design

Session 11

Filled ==our hearts== Acts 14:17

Let me ask a question to three things

    A potato

    A pig

    A person

        What is 2 plus 2?

            Of the three, which one is going to answer the question?

        Why?

What does a person, a pig and potato have in common?

    They all have physical bodies.

What does a person and a pig have that a potato does not?

    The breath of life

    A brain

What does a person have that a pig and potato don't have?

    A heart, (not the physical kind) soul, mind, will and conscience

What does Ephesians 3:17 teach about the heart?

Consider these quotes:

"The heart of man is vulnerable to negativity, but it could be easily fortified with positivity"
― Michael Bassey Johnson

"The heart of man is very much like the sea, it has its storms, it has its tides and in its depths it has its pearls too." ― Vincent van Gogh, <u>The Letters of Vincent van Gogh</u>

"Ah, when to the heart of man Was it ever less than a treason to go with the drift of things, To yield with a grace to reason, and bow and accept the end of a love or a season?" — Robert Frost

Does God have a heart? 1 Samuel 13:14; Acts 13:22

Does man have a heart?   Acts 2:37; Matthew 6:21; 15:19-20; Mark 7:21-23

Does having a conscience, and moral choice, prove that humans were created (1 Peter 4:3) by God, who has a conscience and moral choice? (Matthew 5:45; Romans 9:15)

Let me interview my cat about things that are right or wrong! About good and evil? A lot of people don't believe in God because of all the evil in the world. How do we decide that something is good or evil? What is the standard?

What do these passages teach about the conscience?

    1 Samuel 25:31

        What can happen to the conscience?

    Job 27:6

        How does the conscience reproach?

    Acts 24:16

        What did Paul strive for with his conscience?

        He wanted his conscience clear before whom?

    1 Corinthians 4:4

        A clear conscience does not make a person what?

        Who is our Judge?

        How does this relate to Isaiah 33:22?

1 Corinthians 8:7-12

> According to this passage, what can the conscience be?

2 Corinthians 1:12

> According to this passage, what does the conscience do?

1 Timothy 1:5

> What three things does love come from?
>
> How does Paul describe the conscience?

1 Timothy 4:2

> What can happen to the conscience?

Mankind has a reflective consciousness. In other words, "You know what you know." The conscience is amazing with analytical reasoning. When someone tells you to think about it – you can! This is amazing. We may not be able to comprehend things, but we can contemplate them. What does 1 Corinthians 2:9 teach about this?

> Can humans think critically?
>
>> Critical thinking is that mode of thinking — about any subject, content, or problem — in which the thinker improves the quality of his or her thinking by skillfully analyzing, assessing, and reconstructing it. Critical thinking is self-directed, self-disciplined, self-monitored, and self-corrective thinking. It presupposes assent to rigorous standards of excellence and mindful command of their use. It entails effective communication and problem-solving abilities, as well as a commitment to overcome our native egocentrism and sociocentrism.

www.criticalthinking.org/pages/our-concept-of-critical-thinking/411

> Can humans think creatively?
>
> Can the conscience become polluted (James 1:27)?

The heart is probably one of the greatest testimonies of God. The heart is so complicated it is beyond belief. Proverbs 20:5 states, "The purposes of a man's heart are deep waters, but a man of understanding draws them out."

What do deep waters symbolize?

Are a person's thoughts and emotions deep?

How does this relate to Psalm 64:6; Proverbs 18:4; 1 Corinthians 2:11?

The Greek word for "hear"t is: **kardia** (kar-dee'-ah); prolonged from a primary kar (Latin, cor, "heart"); the heart, i.e. (figuratively) **the thoughts or feelings (mind)**. {Emphasis mine}

(Biblesoft's New Exhaustive Strong's Numbers and Concordance with Expanded Greek-Hebrew Dictionary. Copyright © 1994, 2003, 2006 Biblesoft, Inc. and International Bible Translators, Inc.)

This word is found in NIV 570 times is the NIV. It occurs in the New Testament 81 times. The word heart occurs more in the KJV – 830 times. When I think about this, this is really puzzling – that the KJV has the word "heart" that many more times, than the NIV.

The heart is the center of all emotion, intellect, morals and spiritual life. So, are humans bodies that have a heart and soul, or souls and hearts that have a physical body? Biblically, I believe we are hearts and souls that have a physical body. Our heart and soul are the most precious part of us to God. Our hearts and souls are eternal...

The heart is important...It makes us

- Compassionate and loving – the heart gives us the capacity to feel for someone else. Romans 12:10, 15

- Humans have motivation, that comes from the heart. 1 Corinthians 4:5

- We have passion and intellect – what we feel deeply is what drives us, for good and bad. All of these come from the heart.

According to Psalm 13:2, what can humans do? The NIV uses the word wrestle.

    What happens when you wrestle with your thoughts?

    What two things does thought wresting produce?

    How does thought wrestling create sorrow?

    Who is the "enemy" of this passage?

    How does this enemy triumph over people?

Is Winston Churchill correct, "You have enemies? Good. That means you've stood up for something, sometime in your life."

According to Psalm 55:2 what can humans have? The NIV says "my thoughts trouble me"

> What happens when thoughts trouble us?

Mark 12:30 states four things we should love the Lord with. What are they?

> Heart
>
> Soul
>
> Mind
>
> Strength

Do the heart, soul, and mind happen by evolution? Or can only a being with a heart mind and soul create a being with a heart, mind and soul?

What do these passages teach about the heart?

Matthew 22:37

> What does "all" mean?
>
> How do all the Laws and the Prophets hang on these two commands?
>
> How does this relate to Deuteronomy 6:5?
>
> How does this relate to Deuteronomy 10:12; 11:13
>
> How does God test the heart? Deuteronomy 13:3
>
> How does this relate to Joshua 22:5?

Luke 10:27

> What is different in this passage compared to Matthew 22:37?

Deuteronomy 30:6

    What does God do with the heart?

    How would you describe circumcise?

Using the King James Version of the Bible

    Man can be faint hearted Deuteronomy 20:8; Isaiah 7:4; Jeremiah 49:23

Brokenhearted	Isaiah 61:1; Luke 4:18
Tenderhearted	2 Chronicles 13:7; Ephesians 4:32
Hardhearted	Ezekiel 3:7
Merryhearted	Isaiah 24:7
Stiffhearted	Ezekiel 2:4
Proud heart	Proverbs 28:25
Stolen	2 Samuel 15:6

Let's look at the numbers….Choosing three Old Testament books

    Proverbs has 915 verses with 82 heart verses or 9.0%.

    Psalms has 2461 verses with 130 heart verses or 5.3%.

    Ecclesiastes has 222 verses with 32 heart verses or 14.4%.

In the New Testament:

    The physician Luke wrote about the heart in 11 verses.

    In Paul's letter, he uses the word heart in 29 verses.

In closing, what part of this study was:

Science based

Logic based

Evidence Enlightenment

Divine Design

Session 12

The Heart Acts 14:17

What do these passages teach about the heart? (You are not going to get through all of these passages in one hour – choose the ones you like the most)

Psalm 40:8

How do we put God's law in our heart?

How does this relate to Psalm 119:11?

Psalm 4:7

How does God fill our hearts with joy? Acts 13:52; Acts 16:34; Romans 14:17; 15:13; 1 Thessalonians 1:6

Proverbs 20:5

How is the heart, deep water?

What does deep water mean?

Proverbs 14:10

What does "each heart knows" mean?

Deuteronomy 6:4-6

What does it mean to love with all your heart?

Philemon 7, 20

How is the heart refreshed by people?

What does it mean to refresh the heart in Christ?

1 Peter 1:22

    What is the command in this passage about love?

    What is deep love?

    What is the opposite of deep love?

Jeremiah 17:9

    Is the heart deceitful or full of deceit?

    What is another word for deceitful?

Proverbs 4:23

    What does it mean to guard your heart?

    How do you guard your heart?

Proverbs 3:5

    What does it mean to not lean on your own understanding?

    What does it mean to trust in the Lord?

    How does this relate to Isaiah 55:8-11?

Matthew 6:21

    Why is the heart where the treasure is?

Proverbs 23:26

    What is the request in this passage?

    How do we give our heart?

Proverbs 23:12

    What does it mean to apply your heart?

    How do you apply the heart?

Proverbs 23:17

    What should our heart not envy?

    Why would it envy this?

Psalm 51:10

    Can a person create their own pure heart?

    Why or why not?

Matthew 12:34

    What causes words?

Matthew 13:15

    How does a person cause their heart to become calloused?

    Why would a person do this?

Psalm 73:26

    What makes our heart fail?

    What is a heart failure?

    How is God the strength of the heart?

Philippians 4:7

    How does peace guard the heart?

    What else does peace guard?

John 14:27

    What is the command in this passage?

    What troubles the heart?

    Does fear live in the heart?

Psalm 37:4

>From this passage, what does the heart have?

How do you delight yourself in the Lord?

Psalm 9:1

Where does praise come from?

Matthew 5:8

What is the result of a pure heart?

Who makes the human heart pure?

Mark 6:52

What does a hardened heart mean in this passage?

Psalm 19:14

What are meditations of the heart?

Are they thoughts?

Ecclesiastes 9:3

What are the two things found in the heart?

Matthew 15:18-19

What makes words come out of the mouth?

What are the things that come out of the heart in this passage?

Luke 6:45

    What is stored in the heart?

    How is it stored?

    Who stores it?

Proverbs 15:13

    What emotion comes from the heart?

    What crushes the spirit?

Proverbs 17:22

    What is good medicine?

    What is the result of a crushed spirit?

    What are the bones? Is it the physical body?

Psalm 139:23

    What is the request of David found in this passage?

    What does it mean to "test me"?

    Does anxiety come from the heart?

Ecclesiastes 5:20

    What emotion comes from the heart?

Psalm 119:70

    What two things can happen to the heart?

Zechariah 7:10

    Does the heart think?

Zechariah 7:12

> What can we do to the heart?
>
> What is a sign of a hard heart?

Psalm 73:7

> What is caused by the callous heart?

2 Corinthians 6:11-13

> What does it mean to open wide the heart?
>
> Can the heart be closed?
>
> What does a closed heart look like?

Philippians 1:7

> What does it mean "I have you in my heart"?

Truth: The heart of the matter is probably the matters of the heart! The heart is the source of all conversation, emotion, and behavior.

In closing, what part of this study was:

Science based

Logic based

Evidence Enlightenment

Divine Design

Session 13

Filled our hearts with joy Acts 14:17

There is a plethora of joy passages in this session. Discuss the ones that you are most passionate about and relatable to you.

Where does Joy come from?

    Joy from God: 1 Thessalonians 1:6; Romans 14:17; 15:13; Acts 13:52; Psalm 4:7

    Joy from others: Philippians 4:1; 2 Timothy 1:4; 1 Thessalonians 2:20; 3:9

Which are the greater miracles: taste, the seasons changing, music, touch, or God giving us the capacity to enjoy them?

What does 1 Timothy 6:17 teach?

Is enjoyment:

- Physical?
- Intellectual?
- Emotional?
- Social?
- Spiritual?

What would life be like without emotions? What would be missing, what would be created?

What are the benefits of positive emotions on life and health?

What are the benefits of positive emotions during negative times in life (cancer, death)?

Do emotions help us cope with life?

Do emotions make humans more resilient to life?

Which emotions, negative or positive, are superior to the other?

How are emotions like shock absorbers on the car?

Do positive emotions help us do better with stress and help us adapt to life?

Paul expresses joy in this passage, but could he have mentioned any of the fruit of the Spirit as being a testimony of God?

What is the opposite of joy?

- Sorrow
- Sadness
- Grief
- Depression
- Lack of hope
- Despair

These can be caused:

- By self
- By others Psalm 41:9
- By events

Is this our world today?

Consider this quote:

There are three chief things to remember about joy if we want its power to live by. It is the cause, not the effect, of good in our lives. It increases for us through use, because when we speak, think, and act with joy, there is no room for anything else in our lives. We can cultivate joy with material helps and by serving others, turning our attention outward rather than inward, and giving sincere thanks to God for all our blessings.

Retrieved from http://www.unity.org/resources/articles/power-joy

Biblical passages on joy:

Deuteronomy 16:15

    When was the last time we had a seven-day celebration?

    How does understanding God's blessing bring joy?

    Is it difficult to pray for God's blessing? Psalm 115:15

    How does this relate to Numbers 6:22-27?

    Are you surprised when God blesses the work of your hands?

Nehemiah 8:10

    What is linked to the joy of the Lord?

    So what happens if there is no joy of the Lord?

    Why does God give us strength?

    How does this relate to Psalm 29:11?

    How does this relate to Psalm 28:8-9?

Nehemiah 8:12

    Do Christians celebrate with great joy?

    Why is this great joy a great witness?

    When we understand more about the words of the Lord does this bring joy?

    How does ministering to others bring great joy?

    How does this relate to Proverbs 3:27?

Psalm 47:1

    Is "cries of joy" a strange phrase?

    What does Psalm 27:6 teach about joy?

    How does this relate to Psalm 47:5?

    How does this relate to Psalm 98:4?

How does this relate to Zephaniah 3:14?

How does this relate to Revelation 19:1?

Habakkuk 3:17-18

    Does joy depend on what is happening?

    Should joy depend on what is happening?

    What six bad things are happening in the passage?

    How important were these six things?

    Why was Habakkuk joyful?

    How often do we lose sight of God being our Savior?

Job 9:25

    Is this an adequate description of people today?

    What is a "glimpse" of joy?

    How long does a glimpse last?   How does this relate to Job 10:20; 20:5?

    If this is a true mental condition, what emotions would be created?

    Would depression be a result?

Psalms 16:11

    Do people have a difficult time comprehending the presence of God in their lives?

    How does this relate to Psalms 21:6; Acts 2:28?

    Why is understanding God's presence so important to joy and our mental health?

    How does understanding God's path to life bring joy?

    How does God fill us with joy?

    How does this relate to Psalms 19:8; 20:5; 21:1; 119:111?

    Why does God fill us with joy?

Psalms 28:7

> What are the two descriptions of God found in this passage?
>
> What does the word "my" mean in this passage?
>
> How does seeing God in these two images bring joy?
>
> What is the link between trusting God and joy?
>
> What is the link between giving thanks and joy?
>
> What happens when your heart leaps for joy? Luke 1:44; Luke 6:23

Psalms 30:11

> How does God turn our wailing into dancing?
>
> Why does God do this? Is this a witness?
>
> How does God remove our sackcloth?
>
> How does this relate to Ecclesiastes 3:4?
>
> What does it mean that God clothes us with joy? Psalms 86:4; Luke 10:21
>
> Is this joy clothing we put on?

Psalms 51:12

> What does restore mean?
>
> What are some things that restore joy?
>
> What are some things that steal joy? Joel 1:12; Galatians 4:15
>
> What is a willing spirit?
>
> What does sustain mean?

Proverbs 12:20

> What does it mean to promote Joy?
>
> How does this relate to Romans 12:18; 14:19?
>
> Why does promoting Joy bring joy?
>
> What is another word for deceit?

Is it lies?

Would believing lies take away joy?

How does bitterness remove joy from the heart? Proverbs 14:10

What other emotions can remove joy?

Isaiah 49:13

How do the heavens shout for joy?

Is this joy a form of sign language from the heavens?

When the Lord comforts, does that bring joy? Isaiah 51:3

When we recognize that the Lord has compassion on us, does that bring joy? Isaiah 51:3

What is the connection between joy and affliction?

Isaiah 61:7

From an Old Testament story, who received a double portion? (1 Samuel 1:5-8)

What is the connection between joy and shame and disgrace?

Why do we need "everlasting" joy?

Does this type of joy come from the world?

Does shame and disgrace come from the world?

1 Peter 1:8-9

How is joy described in this passage?

Romans 15:13

What does all joy mean?

What are the two other emotions in this passage?

Does all this come from the Holy Spirit?

2 John 1:12

> Why does Paul want a face to face visit?

Luke 15:7

> What happened when they found the lost sheep?

Romans 14:17

> What are the three effects of the Holy Spirit found in this passage?

Hebrews 12:2

> What was the joy set before Jesus?
>
> Was it the humanity he was dying for?

Luke 2:10-11

> What brought joy to the earth?

Matthew 13:44

> Why did finding this treasure bring joy?
>
> Is this treasure salvation?
>
> Is this treasure heaven?
>
> How do you keep the joy of heaven alive?
>
> What squelches the joy of heaven?
>
> When you think about heaven, does it bring joy to your heart?

John 15:11

> When did Jesus speak this statement?
>
> How does Jesus give us his joy?
>
> Do we understand that we can have the joy of Jesus?

Why is complete joy important while we live on this earth?   John 16:24; 17:13

So can the joy of Jesus become our joy?

How does this transformation take place? John 17:13

John 16:20-22

What would make the disciples weep?

What turned their grief to joy?

What does it mean no one will take away our joy?

Who tries to steal our joy?

What events try to steal our joy?

2 Corinthians 7:4

What three things did Paul feel for the church at Corinth?

How can joy come from or through trouble?

How does this relate to 2 Corinthians 4:16-18?

How do we fix our eyes on Jesus and not our problems?

How do we see problems as light and momentary?

Philippians 2:1-2

What four things mentioned by Paul made his joy complete?

Which of the four is the most difficult to maintain?

What five traits did Paul want the church to possess?

How does encouragement of others bring us joy?

How does tenderness and compassion of others bring us joy?

2 Timothy 1:4

How do people fill us with joy?

What does it mean to recall a person's tears?

Why do you think Timothy had tears?

How does this relate to Philemon 7?

How does this relate to Acts 20:35-21:1?

1 John 1:1-4

What did they write about that made their joy complete?

Was it that they had seen the Life?

What would have happened if they did not write about this joy? (Jeremiah 20:9)

Why did they want to have fellowship?

Does fellowship bring joy?

2 John 4

As a parent, is this true for you?

What truth does John mean here? John 14:6

Why does Father God command us to walk in truth? 3 John 3

Did John see people he ministered to as his children?

Why is this a good analogy?

Jude 24

Who is the him referred to in this passage?

What does it mean to keep us from falling?

How does God keep us from falling?

What are the two conditions of being in God's glorious presence?

Which of the two is the most difficult to conceive?

Galatians 5:22-23

Why does God's Spirit give us the fruit of joy?

Is joy attractive to building and blessing relationships?

Is joy a "shock absorber" for the rough ride of life?

Why does God's Spirit give all of these traits?

Does joy come when love and peace are present?

Philippians 1:4-6

What does it mean to pray with joy?

From verse 6 why was Paul confident?

How did this confidence bring joy?

What is the "day of Christ Jesus'?

Why should the second coming of Jesus bring joy?

Philippians 4:1

How did Paul describe these Philippians?

How does this relate to 1 Thessalonians 2:19-20?

Which of these six descriptions is the most amazing?

Does standing firm in the Lord produce joy?

Is this joy immediate or eternal joy?

Why is there an exclamation mark at the end of this passage?

Romans 12:12

What is the connection between joy and hope?

If I am patient in affliction, does that produce joy?

If I am faithful in prayer, does that produce joy?

Which is the most difficult to maintain, joy, hope, patience or faithfulness?

How does this passage relate to 1 Thessalonians 5:16?

Is this supernatural? Is this eternal? Is this great joy?

In closing

Why does God give us these seven testimonies? Obviously, all of them are needed for our existence…but there is another reason…

Let's look one last time at Acts 14:17

"Yet he has not left himself without testimony: He has shown kindness by giving you rain from heaven and crops in their seasons; he provides you with plenty of food and fills your hearts with joy."

How is God described? God is kind! God has a hand on our lives and he is real! He showed kindness by giving us what we need to live on this planet

Look up:

Ephesians 2:7

Titus 3:4-6

Nehemiah 9:17

The phrase "Lord Almighty" (El Shaddai) is found in the Bible 264 times in the NIV translation. God shows His might by these seven testimonies. We need to be in awe of these seven testimonies!

Never forget why we are here. God gave us our time and place on this planet (Acts 17:26). We are God's witnesses (Acts 1:8; Isaiah 43:10, 12; 44:8). Mark 13:11 has an amazing promise of God when you are speaking or giving your testimony, "Whenever you are arrested and brought to trial, do not worry beforehand about what to say. Just say whatever is given you at the time, for it is not you speaking, but the Holy Spirit." God will speak through you. God is a great teacher and we need to be great students who are always doing continual education!

www.ingramcontent.com/pod-product-compliance
Lightning Source LLC
Chambersburg PA
CBHW081235170426
43198CB00017B/2767